Bravo Alpha Elevens
A Manual For Life

R. K. Taylor

CP

Cadmus Publishing
www.cadmuspublishing.com

Copyright © 2022 R. K. Taylor

Published by Cadmus Publishing
www.cadmuspublishing.com
Port Angeles, WA

ISBN: 978-1-63751-272-2

TABLE OF CONTENTS

Foreword and Disclaimer

We live in a world of ever changing enemies. What used to be reserved for military and police use is now widely available to anyone, anywhere, regardless of their intentions. You can look online right now and find police uniforms, military uniforms, boots, duty belts, OC spray, stun guns of all sorts, expandable batons, military and police radios, siren systems, red and blue lights, and all of the training manuals to go with all of it. Body armor and helmets are widely available from a broad range of retailers, most of which are far superior to the government's lowest bidder options. For a few hundred dollars, anyone can become any three letter agent. These materials are bought in astronomic numbers by doomsday preppers, pseudo-commando rednecks, right and left wing extremists, and a vast number of gang members. Most of these organizations have many in their ranks who are willing to die for their cause, all it takes is for you to be in opposition to their cause and you will soon meet their wrath.

Businesses hide behind background checks as an all-inclusive shift of liability. Background checks are useless as they don't reveal someone's intentions, only whether or not they've previously committed a crime. Sometimes, these background checks only reveal information that would disqualify someone from owning a firearm, such as a felony. Some states allow felons to own firearms as long as their felony was not violent. Simply put, a background check does not let a firearms dealer know that the person buying a firearm is an absolute, homicidal lunatic. Look at several of the nation's mass shooters from 1990 to 2020. Most of these shooters had no disqualifying factors whereas others had severe mental instability or were already on the radar of federal three letter agencies. Clearly, even when the feds know someone is an absolute danger, they cannot act on suspicion. No matter what someone's life looks like, the federal government cannot prohibit the exercise of the Second Amendment rights without due process.

A step beyond a background check is a psychological evaluation. However, many of the most successful CEOs in the nation are psychopaths but are entirely law abiding. Psychological factors, even psychopathy in itself, cannot reflect that a person will become dangerous. Further, psychology, sociology, and social psychology textbooks are available to anyone. With these, anyone to include our nation's most violent offenders, would be able to pass a psychological evaluation. Anyone that has a copy of the DSM-5 or the ICD-10 can readily pass one of these exam-

inations based on knowing what each question references in regard to disorders.

We have to face reality. Everyone we encounter could be the most helpful person, an insane serial killer, an out of control manipulator, or someone simply wanting to take everything you own through years of chess-like manipulation. Each individual has their own flaws and as we are all human, we all have the power to be as good or as bad as anyone that ever lived. There's no clear indicator that someone is about to blow themselves up in the diner next to you or shoot up your church. Active shooters can be anyone from a bullied school child, a person wanting to top the last mass shooter kill score, a recently fired employee, all the way to a radicalized religious nut who's simply killing in the name of their god.

Regardless of the threat, does it matter what they were shooting for once your family is dead? Does it matter whether the gun or bullets that killed your family were legal or illegal? Absolutely not. The only thing that matters is being able to accurately identify these types of threats before they happen.

At any given moment, any situation can turn deadly. A lunatic can pull out a gun over anything and begin wildly spraying bullets all over the place. You'll quickly see open or concealed carriers draw their firearms and begin firing back at the threat, resulting in panicked fire from all parties in all directions. If there's law enforcement near, they may not even be engaging the true threat. They may simply engage the closest person to them who is armed. When high stress situations erupt, everyone is subject to die. Even the innocents at the hands of scared or poorly-trained police.

That badge is not a symbol of omnipotence or skill. We've all seen the video of the break-dancing FBI agent who fired his pistol while dropping it. We've seen wrongful deaths at the hands of police in the news. Everyone has emotions and makes mistakes, to include those with lawful authority. Then, we have the issue of police brutality and abuse of authority. You may be doing everything correct and get in the way of an officer looking to shoot someone that day. Some are under trained and simply don't know the right answer whereas others are overly trained. One will overlook major factors while the other is whole heartedly convinced that your morning coffee may, in fact, be liquid explosive that you're smuggling. There's no limit to the stupidity that one may endure at the hands of an angry cop. As emotions run hot, tempers flare, and stress gets mixed in, mistakes will happen and then they try to cover it up, even if it leads to your wrongful conviction.

It is also common to have groups of criminals pose as law enforcement to rob their rival groups or drug dealers. They don't stick to just their rivals; they often try to impersonate law enforcement to prey on law abiding citizens that will submit to their perceived authority. Will you be able to know the difference between a real cop and a well-dressed thug? Or will you realize when it's far too late, as they're driving away with your cuffed wife and daughter?

The scary thing is that most of the law enforcement manuals are widely available to everyone. This is good in the aspect of being able to know correct police procedures in order to overturn wrongful convictions and win lawsuits, but this same information can be used to impersonate even the highest levels of law enforcement. Granted, you will rarely see anyone be able to fool a peer, as some things you only learn on the job, but the general public is much easier to fool. The difference between a criminal dressed as a cop who intends to rob you and a real cop wrongfully detaining you is only a matter of your rights to address it. If you know for certain it's a criminal impersonating a law enforcement officer, most states will allow you to shoot them on the spot without serious repercussions. A real cop wrongfully detaining you is a whole new subject. Should you ever be at the mercy of a dirty cop who intends to rob you, some states allow you to shoot in self-defense, stand your ground to defend your property, or resist an illegal detention. However, the laws of each state differ. If you begin to notice anomalies with an officer, you activate your hazard lights and call 911. You only stopped once the dispatcher confirmed that it was a real officer behind you. This was problematic for a while, especially in towns with small populations. The town police vehicle was often an unmarked pickup truck or an old rust bucket.

While your rights vary state by state, it's important to know the laws of where you are, where you plan to travel, and the federal laws that go along with it all. Following a state law could have you hemmed up by the feds in a heartbeat. It's only through knowing the laws that you'll be able to assert a valid defense in court.

These types of situations became all too real for me over the course of my first deployment. During a complex attack (when the enemy uses a combination of attacks at the same time) against our small encampment in the Khyber Pass, we were attacked by what we all thought was responding Afghan police. At roughly six in the morning, the truck yard across highway 7 began exploding. Entire tractor-trailers were erupting into fireballs as a result of incoming rocket fire and placed IEDs. Within minutes, roughly a dozen men dressed as Afghan Border Police and Afghan Uniform Police began moving across the wadi (sort of a dry riverbed that makes up large portions of Afghan terrain) and then they dispersed. Not more than a minute later, our perceived friends were slamming us with direct fire from their AK-47s and launching under-barrel grenades at us. If we hadn't been paying attention, this could have gone very badly as a small team of them were attempting to get over our outer perimeter. Thanks to two Apache gunships, a B1B Lancer, and a lot of firepower, we repelled their advance.

No matter what happens, even what you perceive as police help can quickly turn menacing. This book will teach you the basics and the extremes to defending yourself. Whether standing your ground against a mugger, engaging an active shooter with lethal force, or turning your home into a fortress, this book covers it. The "what if" game is too rarely played but is vital to expanding your creativity. Your imagination is the limit when it comes to home defense, just as the enemy's ability to breach it rests in their imagination. This book will make you think, conduct your own research, and hopefully teach you things that will pull you away from the brink of death when you need it the most.

It is important to note that this book is intended to teach you preparation and home defense against the most serious of threats. When society collapses and platoon sized elements want to get into your home, this is the book to reach for. These trained and disguised criminals will be everywhere. Perhaps the former SWAT team is now doing house raids in order to secure their own survival, perhaps former federal agents are using their past knowledge to conduct major heists, perhaps former cops are using breach tools and their knowledge to create havoc on the general public. This is the book you should reach for.

It is also noteworthy that all knowledge is neutral. It is only good or bad when it's applied for that purpose. This book encompasses a lot of crucial survival skills that, if wrongfully applied, will draw immediate attention from every three letter federal agency or land you in a prison cell. This book will not teach you how to construct any explosive, as even discussing such a subject is illegal under 18 USC 842. To obtain a federal conviction under that, the discussed device need not even function, so hold your tongue and never mention such a subject.

When "engaging" is talked about throughout this book, it references engaging a threat with lethal force to defend your life and property, in accordance with local and federal law. A threat that presented itself to you and is immediately threatening your life and property. Lethal force is always a last resort. You'll see plenty in this book to deter any criminal before it even gets to that point, like the firehose OC dispenser or the full lawn zapper that we'll discuss later.

Before we begin, it's important that you understand who your author is and where the knowledge, experience, and tricks come from.

Introduction to the Author and the Material

To give you a quick overview of my life, I'm going to skip around in the areas that built me into the man that I am today. As a child, I was constantly exposed to weapons, domestic violence, suicide attempts, mental games, and I still remember looking down the barrel of a shotgun at three years old. My mother was and is a hard working woman who taught me well and always provided for me. Since she was a working single mother, I spent much of my before and after school time in various daycare centers.

It wasn't until JROTC that I learned that I had a warrior spirit and a natural leadership ability. I quickly became fixated on the military life-style, and I succeeded when I applied myself. Since my freshman year, I worked hard on my physical lifestyle. Hiking, biking, kayaking, rock climbing, rappelling, shooting, and general teenage shenanigans became second nature to me. I ran track and cross country which instilled a lot of values into me. As part of my new lifestyle, I insisted on living out in the back yard in a tent for a summer and every summer after that was filled with camping, going to various summer camps, airsoft and paintball wars, hiking out to various hunting camps, and shooting. I had my first taste of freedom after my freshman year at Saint John's Northwestern Military Academy. I was hooked.

During my Sophomore year, I was promoted to Cadet Master Sergeant, and I was the NCOIC of the S-4 (logistics and supply) shop for my battalion. The summer following, I went to a summer camp in Itasca, Minnesota then spent the rest of it nocturnally. A friend and I would sleep all day, ride bikes all night, have airsoft wars all over town (sometimes roof top to roof top), see what kind of places we could get into, and even rappelled from the AH-1 helicopter at the Hurley police department. That summer was also my first road trip across the country. In me, the warrior spirt was well nurtured by my newfound freedom.

During my Junior year I was promoted to Cadet Second Lieutenant and then First Lieutenant, still in the S-4 shop but now I was the OIC. This year planted the seed of manipulation in me. Once I learned how the property system worked, how to network, coordinate, and plan, I knew that anything can be done. I realized that even the tightest of systems have major flaws and personal integrity is all that stands between you and easy money. This was a skill I'd later use in the Army to pilfer everything from live hand grenades, armor piercing ammunition, off the books commo equipment, and a ton of other gear. Believe me, once the government found this out in 2017, they were not pleased with me.

This kind of thing often begins with a government employee that either is undertrained to recognize the problem or recognizes it but is simply too lazy to intervene. Some, in fact, are also doing what you are and will hide your efforts in exchange for your hiding of theirs. All they have to do is "prove" that they're the only person who can do that sort of job and it brings them job security, free reign, and a lack of accountability.

My senior year, I was a Cadet Lieutenant Colonel and the Battalion Commander of Red Devil Battalion. I started a drill team which conducted armed and unarmed drill as well as armed and unarmed trick drill. I turned grunts and various other noises into drill commands that my highly skilled team executed in unison. This year went very fast. I married and shipped to basic training within ten days of each other, all shortly after graduating high school.

Throughout high school, I worked as a busser and a dish washer at a fine Italian restaurant. Washing dishes taught me that the faster you get the job done, the faster you get to go home. There was no point in manning a job position with tons of down time, so I really enjoyed having free reign to get things done, clean the kitchen at the end of the night, and be on my way. As a busser, I learned how to politely work with others and the importance of networking. The restaurant was a social hub for all of the important people around town and a meeting place for several groups of power. Having the right impression connected me to some very well off individuals who supported my endeavors.

Once I got into the Army on June 12, 2012, I arrived at the 30th Adjutant General's Battalion at Fort Benning. After the two weeks of medical processing, pay processing, and everything that goes along with military entry, I found myself on a white bus headed for Fox Company 1-50. The same company which trained Shughart and Gordon who would later become Delta Operators and sacrifice their lives in Mogadishu, Somalia. Black Hawk Down was made with them at the center of the action. I'll spare you the details of basic training and the OSUT portion of what we do. You can simply go online and watch a video of how infantrymen are made. I graduated on September 27, 2012, and was at my first duty station on October 15, 2012, after Hometown Recruiting orders. I was now at Fort Polk, LA. The meatgrinder of careers.

I was now a part of Chaos Company 2-30 Infantry in the 4th Brigade 10th Mountain Division. The new guy shenanigans (which many call hazing now) were widely practiced but I adapted well. I was a beast in PT, but rucking kicked my ass at the time. This went on for roughly nine months until I found myself on a plane to Afghanistan. I was assigned as the Designated Marksman and backup RTO. We left on July 8, 2013, flying through Germany and Kyrgyzstan on the way there. We spent roughly two weeks at Manas Air Base in Kyrgyzstan doing all sorts of counter IED training. Once we flew into Bagram Air Field, we received in-depth training from Task Force Paladin, one of the world's leading "Counter-IED" Task groups. We flew a C-130 to Jalalabad Air Field, also known as FOB Fenty. From there, we took Sikorsky S-61s out to a small base in the Khyber Pass named Fire Base Torkham. We were now in control of the Khyber Pass. Through our time there, we took hundreds of 107 mm rockets, lots of mortars, and two complex attacks against our base. The first was on September 2, 2013, and the second, which I earned my Combat Infantryman's Badge and an Army Commendation Medal for, was on December 18, 2013.

For the most part, we escorted high ranking individuals out to the Pakistan Border, and we were a Personal Security Detail/Security Escort Team for the Customs and Border Protection's Border Management Task Force. Aside from that, we'd sit in on Key Leader Engagements as Guardian Angel. We also climbed mountains just for the fun of it and to do mortar registration. We returned from this deployment just as we had left, no casualties and a bunch of awards. We got to stop in Romania for a bit and that place is one of the coldest places I've ever visited. We flew into Alexandria, LA on March 4, 2014, at roughly nine at night. That is when the training cycles began again. We had non-stop ranges and training. We were stuck on an Opposing Forces (OPFOR) rotation to help get the 101st Airborne ready for their deployment and got stuck doing Red Cycle Tasking. My part of Red Cycle was an assignment to the 519th Military Police Battalion. I worked the Access Control Points with the 219th Military Police Company and the 258th Military Police Company. That was a blast while it lasted, and I got to closely explore the different personalities that both help and plague federal law enforcement. I learned that there are good, there are bad, there are lazy, there are incompetent, and there are grossly over-trained types.

Shortly after that assignment, we went into live fire training once again. I was moved up in the world to the platoon RTO (Radio Telephone Operator) position. Essentially, I carried multiple radios for the platoon leader and assisted him with anything that he needed. During live fire cycle, my Company Commander saw how efficiently I could call in a 9-line Medevac Request while at a dead sprint. Soon, he made me the communications NCOIC for the company. At that point, I was "King of the Nerds." That's where I learned the property game and how to network between battalions to get everything my company needed. I started working alongside an S-6 technician who expanded my knowledge into Network Communications and helped me get my Communications Security Courier card.

After months of nerdery, I once again found myself on a plane to Afghanistan, assigned as a grenadier. This time, we stopped in Kuwait on the way there for about a week which is hotter than hell itself. We went from Kuwait to Bagram, where we learned the Mk. 44 minigun, the Mk. 47 grenade machinegun, and the Carl Gustaf recoilless rifle. I hit the gym for about an hour before my platoon sergeant told a few of us to pack up, we're leaving. We boarded a small bus which took us to a private twin engine plane on the airfield. This was entirely new. Once we got to Kandahar, we made our way to the headquarters element of 19th Special Forces Group. Immediately, myself and a couple of others piled into a vehicle and drove out to a small ODA camp just outside of Kandahar Airfield. While unpacking, two bearded E-7s came up to me "Welcome to Camp Simmons, kid. You're part of ODA 9114." I found out that they were the National Guard Special Forces Group that covers the whole west coast. The next few months were spent doing some amazing training, some hellish work, and some agonizing hours. In November, we went on a month long hell mission in Helmand Province. We touched through Lashkar Gah, Marjah, and the surrounding villages. It was wild, I learned how shit actually gets done, and that the Regular Army ways are not mandatory. These bearded badasses know exactly how to get the job done and keep things moving. We accomplished a lot while out there and we were lucky to take no casualties. On missions after that, we had a dude named Jess get shot and our team sergeant got shot. ODA 9115 had a dude that got shot in the leg and McClintock was killed while out in Marjah.

A couple of weeks after we got back to Kandahar, eighteen enemies followed us and decided to blow up the bazaar. They begin a complex attack on Simmons and Kandahar Airfield. Needless to say, they all died on December 13, 2015. You can still see pictures of them online. Right after this, we started closing down Camp Simmons which took about a month. I was the last person to step out of there. I grabbed the equipment from the ECP tower, hopped into an SUV and we were on our way to Kandahar Airfield. We were there until the groups rotated in January of 2016.

The middle of January is when 19th Group switched out with 7th Group out of Eglin, Florida. Our platoon pushed out to a new camp in Helmand, and I got moved up to Kabul. Our small camp was near the King's palace, Darulaman Palace, and the Parliament Palace. I was then part of ODB 7220. We got a lot more range time, had regular workout routines scheduled, and did a ton of static security. It was a very relaxed assignment, and the only real excitement was when myself, an Air force Captain, a JFO, and an interpreter had to go inventory part of the Afghan Commandos compound. We were three seconds from a green-on-blue at their gate and I was ready to cook us all with a frag. The Afghans snapped to the ready when we pulled up, strong walling across our vehicle with M-4 and M-16 rifles. The terp wouldn't get out of the truck and an Afghan commander pulled me out of the passenger seat of the vehicle. Luckily, our terp nutted up and my calm demeanor stabilized the situation. Shortly after that, on March 29, 2016, we had a rocket attack on the Parliament Palace where one round fell short. It hit close enough to daze me with no serious injuries. The round destroyed our good MWR, the barber shop, and three shipping container buildings. I had black eyes for a couple of days and a hell of a headache for about a week.

The deployment from that point on was getting ready to leave in June. The workouts were good, the food was amazing, and the range time was priceless. I spent my off time tanning in a purple thong while smoking a pink hookah, the selfies were priceless but probably horrifying to the young ladies who received them. In the beginning of June, we pushed back to Kuwait to begin the tanning/pool phase of the deployment. We lathered up in bronzer and hit the poolside.

On June 18, 2016, we got back to the US at roughly lunch time and that's where all the real fun began.

I had eighteen thousand dollars in the bank, a ton of new tactical equipment that I'd been ordering to Kim's house for the whole deployment, and I literally restarted my life. After a short inventory period of about an hour, we decided to head down to the Class Six which is the on-post liquor store. There, I met my first post-deployment girlfriend. A gorgeous strawberry blonde who was giving out samples of a new strawberry ale. We stocked up on beer and liquor then headed back to go through all of my stuff thoroughly.

I had a new plate carrier, soft armor, new AR parts, a set of generation 4 AN/PVS-14s (monocular night vision device), two new ACH ballistic helmets with base plate and rhino mounts, an AN/PEQ-15, tons of new 15 and 17 round Glock magazines, 20 and 30 round AR mags, tons of new clothes (regular and tactical), a whole vehicle emergency kit with fire extinguishers, a medic's aid bag, a roadside emergency kit, and then started buying guns. Buying and trading guns has always been one of my hobbies and I moved up in the world to assembling ARs piece by piece at gun shows.

Life became a non-stop party since all my bills were paid, the ex-wife was at bay, and I was prepared for anything and everything. J, the pretty red-head from the class six turned out to be a very cool person and originally from Grand Rapids, Michigan. We went wine mudding in her jeep and drove all over the Fort Polk trail systems. We had a lot of fun but due to our fast paced lives, our relationship didn't last very long.

When I got back from post-deployment leave, it was non-stop training. We went hard and we went non-stop. I'd spend a week or two in the field, come back to a new girlfriend, spend another week or so out there, come back to another girlfriend, EIB training, new girlfriend, driver's training, new girlfriend, month long box rotation, new girlfriend, OP-FOR rotation, new girlfriend. The cycle went on like this until right before I got locked up. As you can see, I was an ardent rake.

I attended plenty of college parties at LSU, NSU, SOWELA, and wherever the Greeks were partying.

At one of those Greek nights, the DJ made my buddy's girl cry, and I simply went over to where they were talking. Evidently, I was a bit too aggressive, and he had to keep telling me to get out of the DJ booth and begged me not to do anything stupid. He tried to convince me that "my stripes aren't worth it." Little did he know, I was an E-4 and didn't give a shit. Long story short, security (college idiots in Sperry shoes) sternly persisted at removing me from the DJ booth, where I persisted in scaring the hell out of the national guard college boy working there. As we went to check on M, we noticed Natchitoches police pulling into the parking lot and decided that it was best for me to return to my daiquiri from the drive-thru liquor store.

I'd had plenty of these encounters all over Lake Charles, Baton Rouge, Lafayette, Slidell, Natchitoches, Shreveport, and the small towns no one ever heard of.

I was on leave again when I met the gorgeous Kay Jewelers manager who was opening up her own store east of Baton Rouge. We had a ton of fun, went hotel hopping all over Louisiana (she lived hours away in Mississippi), explored all over Baton Rouge, and had a wonderful relationship until interruptions happened.

Aside from my shenanigans and lecherous endeavors, I liked to train in my free time. I spent every extra dollar I had on weapons, ammo, and new toys. My roommate was a complete Geardo, and I followed suit. With my 2008 Toyota Corolla and 2002 Ford Ranger, I'd practice all sorts of drills. Mounted firing, dismounted firing, firing from each position of the car and from each window, skidding to stops, drifting onto the range, practicing rear attacks, and multi-gun shooting.

I got scary good and could engage targets all around the vehicle, change weapons (roughly two ARs, a shotgun, and three pistols) while alternating directions, and then the other toys came in.

Obviously, I've done some wrong in my life and it involved explosives. The Feds hammered my ass for it, too. One of my hobbies was building large versions of fireworks, homemade grenades to incorporate at the range, and there was the theft of several high ticket items from the Army. I'll tell you one thing though, the second they began an investigation, they found everything. My roommate even drew them a map of the apartment and where all of my stuff was. Turns out, all I had to do was file the proper ATF paperwork and I could have legally bought all of that through official channels. Well, here I sit in prison due to my recklessness, really disregard for the laws. However, I never thought that homemade Tannerite would land me a chemical weapons charge. I made sure that the recipe wasn't an energetic nor an explosive, so I thought I was good to go under US law. Well, I was, until they brought in the International Chemical Weapons Convention and showed that my cook process produced Chlorine Gas, which is a highly volatile substance listed as a Weapon of Mass Destruction, for which I got a two-point sentencing enhancement.

I urge you not to do this sort of thing, ever. Know the laws, even the ones you think could never cover your conduct, if they want you, they'll get you.

Aside from this, I was the trustworthy go-to guy because of my known stability and my knowledge of how to apply pressure to individuals to make them stop their shenanigans. On more than one occasion, I was summoned by my female friends who had dead-beat men plaguing their life. Some of these were simply pick them up and get them out of the situation. Others got rough very quick. I had to maintain a calm demeanor to keep the situation from spilling into the uncontrollable side. For the women that I was involved with, I'd pose as the gay friend. Since I'm 140 pounds standing at an ominous five-foot, five-inches tall, it was rather easy to don a pink polo shirt and assume the role when getting them away from their loser boyfriends.

On one occasion, my quick draw from the appendix carry saved my life. This chick, we'll call L texted me to pick her up in a hurry. I cruised out to her place, a small Texas style adobe house, with the lights off and the truck in neutral. The house was dark, so I went around back. As her bedroom light was on, I could see from the window that she was passed out on the bed. I went in through the back door and slowly nudged her door open. This dude was lying next to her in the bed, and she was nude from the waist down. I poked her quietly in the face. No response. I crept in and slowly began to lift all ninety pounds of her off of the bed when the dude wakes up. He begins to swing a shotgun around to me and I simultaneously drop L back to the bed, pull out the Glock 19 from my waistband and gain control of the situation and the shotgun. Cradling both the unconscious L and the shotgun, I flew out the back door and got the hell out of there. Turns out, she popped four Xanax bars when the police pulled her car over. Wild times.

Aside from this, I've almost gotten into three gunfights outside of the Leesville Walmart (the youngsters were rowdy in 2016 and each of them had guns), nearly had to use my firearm in a road rage incident in Lake Charles, I've stopped a suicide attempt, been the first responder to a fatal motorcycle-deer collision, gotten friends away from pissed off husbands, scared off drug dealers, handled several domestic violence situations, and I continue to be ready for anything. I'm not sure whether I was simply more in-tune with problems due to deployments or whether the world really did deteriorate after my second deployment. Regardless, I think I made a huge difference in some people's lives.

It's through times like this that I learned how vulnerable people can be, even from those that are supposed to love them. Situations can quickly go awry and even turn deadly at the drop of a hat. The only person you can control in this world is you, everyone else is a major variable.

Within a year of coming back from my second deployment to Afghanistan, emphasis on second time, I found myself in my current legal troubles. I was indicted in 2017 on 18 USC 229 Use of a Chemical Weapon. I quickly learned what it was like to be at the mercy of dangerously under-trained law enforcement, many of which required no training to serve as a jailer. Major security flaws were everywhere, there were compromised staff, and absolute scum bags in uniform. While in Louisiana, I was locked up in Vernon Parish, Calcasieu Parish, and Lafayette Parish. There's good and bad staff in each one of those. Some of which, out of their ignorance, caused and allowed several serious injuries to occur. Simple tells in their body language revealed key information as to who the government informers were and that jeopardized several peoples' safety. Inmates are cunning species, masters of deception, and apply a level of "street-smarts" that can manipulate people in ways you'd never imagine. Rookie staff are extremely vulnerable and constantly exploited by those in the know.

Prison is where non-criminals go to learn the skills to do the rest of their life in prison. Before prison, I was pretty well trained across a broad range of skills. Since being locked up abroad, I've learned far more advanced fighting skills than I'd ever learned in the Army. I've been locked up with bank robbers, meth cooks, murderers, contract killers, computer criminals, pedophiles, thieves, fraudsters, embezzlers, burglars, safe crackers, pimps, RICO criminals, and all other sorts of people that will readily tell you everything about their trade-craft. It's a melting pot where horrible people go to make each other worse. Incarceration itself harms society more than if the criminals were still on the streets. At least then, they wouldn't train others to get away with it "next time." Half the people in here look forward to getting out to pull off a crime in a more complex manner. All they care about is faking out the government long enough to get mildly rich.

However, we can choose to apply ourselves differently. I've become a Certified Production Technician, Certified Logistics Associate, Fork

Truck Operator, and a Paralegal. All within the three years of prison time that I've done. Over the years, I've had a very broad range of skills available to me and learned a lot. I continue learning all I can across every subject, and I recently invested in books on forging. If you can forge, you can make blades. If you can make blades, you can survive. I've dedicated a lot of time and effort to learning all that I can, and I can only hope that you do the same.

Over the years, life has brought me from Michigan and Wisconsin to Louisiana, Texas, Mississippi, Georgia, Missouri, Illinois, Kansas, Nebraska, Oklahoma, and New York. Overseas, I've been to Germany, Kyrgyzstan, Kuwait, Romania, Afghanistan, and Pakistan. I've worked with all sorts of ethnicities, social backgrounds, financial backgrounds, races, religions, the incarcerated, and groups of people identified by a sign. One thing is for sure, people are people. The good, the bad, the horrifying, we are all human. Respect, courtesy, and knowledge of their cultures will keep you alive and well.

It's your job to get out there and learn all that you can so that you can identify the nefarious angles that people will approach you from. You need to be able to identify a threat, a murderer, a rapist, a pedophile, the career thieves, the swindlers, the scam artist, and the simply insane. By knowing these people, you can develop a course of action to safely handle them, even if it means knowing when to up the gun and defend yourself.

This book will give you a good foundation and a lot of new things to think about. However, I will not give you answers. I will plant ideas into your head that will inspire you to look deeper into the matter. I lay a solid foundation for you to build off of and I tell you where the answers are hidden. By reading the material thoroughly, you will become much smarter, stronger, mentally strong, street-smart, and be better able to survive anything.

This book was not planned. An acquaintance of mine told me after a few hours of my venting, that I should put all of my knowledge into a book. So I did. I sat down, typed this out, and now I'm rolling with it. I hope you enjoy.

Chapter 1

Preparations

Education and the Warrior Entrepreneur

There is a vast array of knowledge at your fingertips and thousands of business opportunities available to you. You should always make your preparations pay for themselves and a business is the best way to do this. Everyone has heard of organized crime rings using a storefront to launder money and have a secure place that seems legal. Well, try to copy them. Get into business that is natural to you, something that you can make money off of, and run with it. The extra profits are a major monetary asset that can be used to further your preparation efforts. Getting into business that helps grow both your profit and your preps will be the single greatest asset you can attain.

Imagine it now, you own your own camping supply shop, kayak and canoe shop, ammunition reloading service, canning business, or any of the other lines of work that facilitate your supply additions. Back in the Army, my profit was the vast availability of excess supplies that could be simply walked away with. Uniforms, helmets, body armor, weapons parts, armor piercing ammunition, tactical gear of all kinds, vehicle supplies, and MREs were all readily available and routinely lost. I was able to hoard without technically stealing.

If you have no idea of what business is best for you, turn your hobby into a money maker. By doing what you love and already do for excitement, you can build your passion into a product. You should never have to pay for your own supplies and by selling a service for profit, you are simply letting your customers pay for your new gear. Look online right now at all of the gear that's sold, who's selling it, where they buy from, and what could be done better. Then ask yourself, "why isn't my name on this label?" This goes for all trades and hobbies. Whatever one man has done, you can also do and it's past the starting point. Perhaps you're tech savvy, good with a machine, can sew, reload ammunition, work on cars, wrap fishing rods, or make lures. Each of these fields give you the opportunity to own your own equipment, put your own personal style into something, and create limitless profit.

Education is your key to success

Even things you have no immediate need for, may come in handy down the road from now. For instance, I'm in federal prison as I write

this, but I've attained a paralegal certificate, certified production technician, certified logistics associate, and fork truck qualifications. Every certification, every piece of knowledge, and every lesson you learn is another round of ammo in your life's magazine. When the fire fight begins,
you'll be glad that you had every round of it. Subjects such as criminolo-
gy, sociology, psychology, social-psychology, elicitation, counter-elicitation, surveillance, counter-surveillance, law enforcement investigations,
private investigations, profiling, body language, nursing and first aid, living off the grid, eating in the wild, carpentry, welding, sewing, knitting,
automotive mechanics, dentistry, gunsmithing, blade smithing, business
management, computer coding, cryptography, and clothing design will
provide you with skills for almost any situation. Study every law enforcement and military manual that you can get your hands on. If I can study
all of this while in prison, you can study it all while out there.

Go Deeper

Go through the police academy, the private investigator's course, get
your paralegal certificate, get your EMT qualification, become a nurse,
go through formal survival courses, get your Concealed Carry Permit,
get range time with a professional firearms instructor, take a precision
driving course, and get as much college as possible. It helps you paint an
accurate picture of who you are, makes you an invaluable asset no matter
where you go, and looks great if you ever get arrested.

But, don't stop there. Once you have your idea of what to do, where
to go, and how to create things for yourself, there's a step further. Learn
extreme couponing, look into the ideas of other doomsday preparers,
and try all of your new skills. You want all of your properties, all of your
supplies, and all of your plans to pay for themselves. While studying,
you'll notice that there are several weaknesses in your existing ideas and
the new knowledge will add much to them. However you can achieve it,
your goal is to have so much money that your preps are paid for from
your abundant profits.

Appearances and Behavior

No matter how good you are at being prepared, don't ever advertise this. You are not a secret agent so do not act like it. Having lots of supplies or living a mysterious lifestyle paint a huge target on you, not only from those who want to rob you but also homeland security. If you don't believe me, look at what happened to the Branch Davidian compound. Once you start being seen with years' worth of food, impenetrable shelters, followers, exotic weapons, and armored vehicles, the feds are either going to label you as a militia or an extremist group, regardless of criminal history or your intentions. The last thing you need is a cop having probable cause to detain you. You might be in violation of a tax law you've never heard of or some local ordinance that no one has used in decades.

You should appear non-threatening. Always conduct yourself in a professional, business-like manner and be presentable. Personally, I used the appearance of a goofy college kid and it helped me fly under the radar.

Looking like a tactical badass puts you in the cross hairs of the other preparers in times of emergency. They'll recognize factors that identify you as one of the few thrivers in times of chaos and they'll want to get to your supplies. The government, which would be in a state of panic, would see a competent threat and could detain you under several provisions of law. You'll see this commonly happen with those who have committed certain crimes, expressed anti-government views, and those who are well prepared for the long fight. In the government's eyes, the only reason to pack thousands of rounds of ammo into a fortress is to fight them. Personally, I wouldn't want them thinking of me in that light and neither should you. Other preparers may also see you as a competent threat and decide to shoot you on sight. Don't be in anyone's sights, be the dude who looks like a pussy and is therefore of no consequence to anyone.

Should you decide to buy your supplies in bulk, always carry your items from your vehicle into your home in regular grocery bags, more so with tactical supplies. The last thing you want to do is be the guy who is unloading several gun cases, a Sparrow's lockpicks bag, Halligan breach tools, and a Barrett m107 in front of neighbors who may later snitch on you.

Furthermore, quit doing illegal things, no matter how slight. Illegal acts of any kind give law enforcement probable cause to enter your home, search whatever they want, and begin confiscation. When the feds raided me, they took every one of my legally owned and registered firearms. It's been five years and they still give me the run-around as to their disposition. This is the last thing you want to happen to you right before the collapse of society. Also, the cops who enter your house may be simply casing the place to come back and rob you later. Anyone that knows what you have is a potential threat to you, your home, your family, and your supplies. Trust no one.

I strongly urge you to hide everything. Your supplies should be tucked away in a neat closet or compartments in your basement, your attic, your walls, or hiding spots that only you know. Don't keep military, police, or survival manuals where anyone can see them.

Your bookshelves should contain regular reading material, cookbooks, gardening, and your books on craftsmanship. These books are innocent and appear normal in the context of a regular home. Your Bookshelf should be some place hidden; this capital Bookshelf is the one that contains your military and police manuals, anarchist's cookbook, improvised munitions book, CIA lockpicking manual, poison dart 101 manual, psyops manual, army guide to booby traps, gunsmithing, blade smithing, and other shady publications. Always keep these books out of view and let no one know that you have them.

Those sorts of books draw attention and can be used by the feds to charge you with Conspiracy.

Your home should look like a normal, happy home. Put up your disco ball, lava lamp, plants, hippie artwork and all of the other beautiful home décor that you want. You'll be glad you did. Appearance is everything to people so if you look like a conspiring lunatic, you'll be treated like one.

When the feds raided me, they were surprised that I wasn't already on some watchlist or even on their radar due to the nature of the equipment that I readily had available.

Training and Field Preparation

To succeed in hard times, you must be a harder person. Get all of the hands-on survival training that you can. Learn to live in hell and learn to love it there. Once you're out on your own, the only thing stopping an enemy from getting to you is your ability to out-think them, out-maneuver them, and to go through things that they aren't willing to. The hot temperatures, the freezing temperatures, the hellish rain, the ridiculous snow, the bugs, and the thorns all play their role in your asset arsenal. Once you learn to live submerged in water, make peace with the bugs, spiders, and snakes, you're on your way to becoming at home in the woods.

Once you do this enough, you'll figure out ways to dry faster, sleep warmer, keep your emotions under control, and embrace the suck. You'll notice that thistle, briars, mesquite, brambles, and roses are more effective than barbed wire at slowing down a threat. You'll learn that nature does not crack sticks, it gets silent in the presence of a predator, you'll learn the sounds of a human, and you'll learn that nothing will cross a five foot deep, five foot wide trench unless it's there to kill you.

While packing, it's important to know that everyone's ruck will be different, but the basics are the same. Food, hygiene, clothing, sleeping gear, essential tools, and toilet needs.

Head down to the sporting goods store and you'll see all sorts of gear that comes in all kinds of fabric. The only way to know for sure what the strengths and weaknesses of each one are is to actually bring it through hell. Only then, will you know which type of that specific item that you want to carry. It's an extremely long process but it's worth it.

When shopping for clothing, pay attention to how it feels, the weight, quality of the stitching, quality of any zippers, and how it wicks moisture. You'll have to make decisions based on this about what environment to use it in. There's simply some gear you use in wet climates that you won't use elsewhere. When certain fabrics get wet, they hold water and get extremely heavy. A forty pound ruck can easily turn into 120 when the wrong things get wet. You'll also know that you won't want winter gear in the summer and vice-versa. Some fabrics breathe well where others are absolutely impermeable. Good equipment in the wrong environment can be a pain in the ass while camping and deadly in a survival situation.

Sleeping bags are a whole new ball game. You'll see all lengths, widths, person capacity, materials, temperature rating, and all sorts of other features. The most important factor of the sleeping bag is the bivy cover. This is the outer windproof and waterproof shell that feels like a soft piece of tarp. This beautiful outer shell keeps you out of the elements of harsh environments. The second piece is the light/summer bag. You want a thin bag that will keep you warm when it gets down to the mid-fifties out there. This bag will generally work well throughout spring, summer and fall. Personally, I used to sleep on top of the bag during the hot Louisiana summer months. You want your light bag to be just that, generally thin and light. Your third layer is your heavy/winter bag. This bag alone is ideal for use between thirty degrees to however cold your area can get. This bag is your fluffy, warm bag for when hell freezes over. Now, this is where it gets important. Your sleeping bags and bivy are a sleep system. Your light bag should fit into the heavy bag and they both should fit into the bivy together. You want to be able to go into maximum cocoon mode for when hell actually does freeze over. By being in both bags and shielded by your bivy cover, there's almost no limitation to how comfortable you can be. If you're frequenting the arctic, your light bag may be a bag rated for zero degrees and your heavy bag to negative fifty degrees. When you cram those into a bivy and use your snow walls correctly, you'll be amazed at how soft, fluffy, and warm you are throughout the night. However, never, ever, once again never, pack things tightly.

The fourth and final part of your sleep system is the sleeping mat. No matter what kind of bags you have, how cool your bivy is, or how much bush craft you know, the earth will suck out your warmth and leave you for dead. You always have to have a barrier between your sleeping bags and the ground. Whether it's a super designed NASA level mat from the best sporting goods store or a thick bed of grass, you need a barrier. Personally, I'd go for the NASA space age sleeping mat. They're light, insanely dense, stay dry, and they're quiet. A pile of grass can have any type of bug or predator crawl into it to feast on you during the night.

A beautiful tip that I learned while in Lashkar Gah was to sleep in your bag naked. I had my heavy bag inside my bivy cover and I was dressed in my poly-pro base layers, my waffle top and bottom, and even my fleece. I froze every night until someone pointed this out. I thought he was nuts. He said to put my boots at my feet and push off all my clothes to the bottom of the bag. I thought he was nuts. Sleeping naked in this cold with my dirty boots and my clothes pushed into a ball at my feet? So, I tried it and I was absolutely amazed. I got the first night of sleep that I had in a week. By keeping your boots and clothes at your feet, it keeps them warm, so you don't have to don freezing clothes and your boots keep air circulation, so your feet don't freeze. Never would I have suspected that the right answer, the simple answer, was to do this.

Toilet articles are the next thing you want to explore. You'll see all sorts of biodegradable toilet paper, portable toilets, and other things to go along with this. Personally, my toilet kit and the toilet kit of every knowledgeable infantryman was the pack of baby wipes and our folding shovel. The baby wipes leave you cleaner, they're durable, and you can bathe with them. Toilet paper is weak, single purpose, and useless when wet. Whether it's humidity, rain, or the sweat off of your body, your toilet paper is going to shred. Any infantryman who has had to use the bush in Louisiana or in a rainstorm can attest to the fact that toilet paper has no place in the military. You can buy ten thousand baby wipes in packs for a few dollars, and they'll be your life saver. Bath wipes are wonderful things for hygiene, but they can be a bit unnecessary.

It also pays to know that high proof liquor is also shampoo and body wash. It will strip body oil off of you when you need it. It also pays to know that baby oil will strip off even the thickest face paint in an instant and a folding canvas chair with a hole cut in it is an amazing portable toilet.

Now, that you've done all of your shopping and exploring, you must try what you've bought. Put each piece to the test and learn its limits, play with it all and learn how it works in each environment. You also do this to get rid of the new gear shine. You want everything to have that tried and true look, so your clothing doesn't light up in the sun and give away your position.

Get it dirty, dusty, sandy, muddy, and keep playing. Get it soaked, cover yourself in mud, and have fun out there while practicing your skills. When it rains, go off and try to use the toilet paper and you'll never pack it again. You'll slowly see what methods work for you, which ones don't, what gear is prone to leak, which clothing articles dry quickly, and which items stay wet and begin to mold.

I'm confident that you'll learn to put all of your socks, t-shirts, and other needed items into freezer bags. I used to put seven pairs of socks into a two-gallon freezer bag and squeeze the air out of it. Now, you have a dense, easy to pack, waterproof sock carrier. I've done this with t-shirts too which helps keep the weight down if it rains.

For the larger items such as pants, jackets, sleeping bags, and other things, you want to have good quality waterproof bags. You can get super thick military issued ones for a few dollars or you can go expensive and get them in all shapes and sizes. Another great item to buy are stuff-sacks.

These have little straps all around it to help you compact your load into dense, space saving packs. Personally while out there, I quit wearing underwear. It binds, rides up, and holds the sweat to your body. The worst time I've ever had was while wearing compression shorts. Yes, it kept everything where it needed to be but after hours of sweating and drying off then sweating more, I quickly developed heat rash in all the wrong places. By "going commando" you allow everything to breathe and have less garments to carry. The last thing you need is the extra pound of underwear which turns into two pounds when sweaty. Remember, when things get dirty, you need a place to put them in your ruck to separate it from everything else. The last thing you want is to have to lug around more dirty items. Yes, you can do laundry out there but that's not practical out of a camp setting.

Now, Let's Get Into Supplies

We'll begin with toys. You'll want a magnesium fire starter, toenail clippers, tweezers, a good pocketknife, a good, fixed blade knife, a short machete, a small hatchet to split wood (not the fighting hatchet), a Bic lighter or ten, a hundred feet of 550 cord, and a folding saw. These items are all you need to live a happy life out in the woods. In this list, I'm assuming that you already have your every day carry firearm and your rifle properly stored nearby.

When it comes to food, you want light-weight, compact, nutritious options that are high in protein. If you get miliary MREs, take out all of the boxes and everything you are not going to use. I used to field strip cases of MREs and put two entrees, two sides, two breads, and two peanut butters/cheese packs all into a freezer bag. I carried twice the food in half the space because of this.

Your next option are the dehydrated meals that you can find at any sporting goods stores. Mountain House is a great company with a lot of options and the military has similar MREs to this which are called Long Range Patrol MREs. By boiling water and adding it to the pack, you have a full hot meal ready to go. They're the best MREs I've ever had in my life. The only thing better are the extreme cold weather MREs which are huge, are packed with carbs, calories, and protein. If you choose to pack these types of meals, you'll need to pack a Jet boil or other similar camping stove. Personally, I love the propane stoves and they work so much faster when you run them on a yellow tank. When packing these meals, you might also consider packing a pot to cook in. You can add several meals to the pot, spice it up with some jerky or other additions, and you'll have the perfect group meal to bond over. When I first started out, I carried a propane torch that I could use to boil water in my canteen cup. That metal canteen cup is amazing but the clang from it can be heard from over a hundred meters away.

When on the move, you want beef jerky, peanuts, peanut butter packs, tuna packs, First Strike meals, protein powders so you can make a shake in a canteen, Clif bars, oatmeal, trail mix, or some of the huge selection of protein bars. Now, Clif has taken a beating by other companies, but I trust them religiously. Yes, they have added sugar, but that sugar will put you into a better mood, help keep fat on your body, and it tastes great. Your diet is up to you but while out in the woods, I prefer to eat happily.

Shelter

You want your shelter to be low to the ground (the roof will be a tarp roughly three feet up at the highest), which will trap your body heat in it. Any higher than that, you just have a wind breaker. A 10' x 10' tarp does amazing for this in an A-frame configuration. Get online and search "Tarp Shelters" and you'll be amazed. You can also get into the wide selection of tents that are available, some of which in single person configurations. These can be absolutely wonderful, but they're easily seen, thin walled, and they can leak if anything touches the sides of it. No matter what you do, you'll want to camouflage your site. Be sure to keep your shelter in an irregular shape. Nothing in nature is geometric or solid color. Brown, tan, olive, or green tarps can easily be spray painted to break up hard lines, accent the high and low spots, and change the pattern. The spray paint will not stick to the tarp though. You'll want to spray the whole thing with spray adhesive and then sprinkle shredded burlap in irregular patterns all over it. Burlap is widely available in all natural colors so jumble up a bunch of small pieces, scrub the new shine off, and adhere it to the tarp. If you're into natural camouflage, you'll have to change out your vegetation daily to keep it fresh. Once things go brown, they'll highlight your position.

Water

Carrying a lot of water is usually not an option. First, you drink it too fast. Second, it's heavy. Before going anywhere, it's important to know where the rivers, lakes, and streams are. Also know where they're at in reference to your bug out locations which we'll discuss in depth later. Be sure that your water source is not an industrial waste pond or a leeching pond. The last thing you want to do is drink waste chemicals or human fecal matter. Look also into what kind of animals frequent that location. You don't want to drink animal waste or find out that your new watering hole is a home to alligators. Some wildlife also carry many bacteria that will seriously harm you or may go through a regular water filter with ease. It pays to carry a portable water filter with you and also have a means to boil it. There are several options available in every sporting goods shop in the nation, so I won't go terribly into detail on this. Most will work effectively as advertised, all you have to do is keep track of how much water goes through it, so you know when to change a filter.

Since we're discussing lakes, streams, and rivers, it's important to mention to always keep a collapsible fishing rod with you. If you don't like these, at least carry fishing line, hooks, and a bobber in your bug out bag. If you can't find bait, find a way to carry the water and dump it into the grass nearby. The earth worms will have to surface to breathe and are then available for the picking. You can try this in your back yard to practice. As long as you can filter water and catch fish, you'll survive for the long haul. In winter times, your trusty ax can hack through the ice on a lake for you to ice fish. Snow, when boiled, is great for dinking. Next is one of the most important subjects.

Medical Supplies

Your most common outdoor injuries are sprains, strains, broken bones from falls, blisters, splinters, debris in the eyes, stomach illness, bites, and burns since you'll have a fire. Don't buy one of those awful, pre-packaged home first-aid kits. They have a lot of unnecessary fodder. Get a waterproof zipper bag to keep your supplies in and make sure you have a nice pouch or pack to put it in. MOLLE systems used by the military have many waterproof pouches that hook onto many existing packs. In your kit, you'll need a pair or two of hemostats, a pair or two of forceps, a scalpel set, suture kits, rolls of two-inch and four-inch kerlix, two-inch and four-inch gauze pads, plastic and metal tweezers, EMT shears, a couple CAT tourniquets, nasopharyngeal airways, a couple NCD needles which are 3.25 inch 14-gauge needles, alcohol prep pads, burn gel packs, hemostatic powder or spray, acetaminophen, ibuprofen, naproxen, Pepto bismol, eye drops, saline, muslin bandages, compression bandages, chest seals, occlusive dressings, bite kits, and a bottle of liquor. In times of actual emergency, go get the most common antibiotics, penicillin, amoxicillin, doxycycline, and a few others to keep on hand.

In addition to the supplies, you must know how to use them all. The American Red Cross and FEMA teach several first-aid courses, courses in CPR, disaster preparedness, and a few others. Get good, be good, stay good, and get better. These things can mean the difference between life and death.

Bug Out Locations

What would you and your family do if you came home to a smoldering pile of rubble? Your clothes, shelter, ability to keep clean, your food, and everything inside are now gone. If you have a vehicle, this may now be your only means of survival. Are you prepared to face this type of reality? Sadly, many people are not and many also do not have a spare vehicle. I used to keep a spare vehicle in my company parking lot that had my full vehicle load out kit, roadside emergency kit, MREs, water, clothes, and blankets in the trunk. The interior always stayed meticulously clean so as not to attract attention, but it was always packed and ready to go. At a moment's notice, I could hop in and get roughly 400 miles on the tank of gas in it. These little preps were in place specifically for these types of problems.

Whether your home was taken out by a jealous rival, electrical fire, gas leak, lightning strike, flooding, or a mortar round, it's gone and it's a reality that you're stuck with. Wouldn't it be nice if you have a solution to this? Perhaps another location to safely evacuate to? This next part is what you should begin doing right now, so if the above mentioned disaster strikes, you're not sitting in your driveway wondering what to do.

A new concept of "home" is long overdue. A house is simply a presentation of your life, your social status, and your personal standards. When you think about it, the average house is a simple 2"x4" skeleton with siding, basic insulation, and drywall, it takes four pounds per square inch to rip your walls down entirely and ruin your house.

You should use your house to paint a picture that you're the average citizen. It's easy as it sounds. You'll use it daily, establish your "neighbor" persona, establish a steady work schedule, and blend in with the others in your area. Forget about showing off, this only paints a target on you to be robbed. We all know the new neighbor who has every new gadget, the new big screen TV in every room, the host of the super bowl parties that shake the neighborhood with their surround sound system, and the ones that have the seemingly always new cars. These people have painted a target on themselves and they, more often than not, do not have the means to defend it. Also, when you continue to host parties, show off new toys, or let people know that you're prepared, they quickly tell others. People you don't even know will soon have the information on what is in your house. This is where the idea of home comes in. Your home is where your family is whether it's in a house, a hunting cabin, or a simple structure out in the woods, your home can be anywhere. This is why it's important not to have an absolute tie to a certain building. Each area that you reside in should have the necessities to live happily but your home is always with you.

I used to have friends over all the time, host dinner parties, and have a good social life. Most of the people over were fellow soldiers and men that I'd served in Afghanistan with. This lifestyle quickly morphed to include their friends, girlfriends, and strippers. Those same friends, even the ones I served in Afghanistan with, quickly told my business, even to the FBI. They told detailed stories of my fully automatic weapons, home-made explosives, and larceny habits. My former roommate even drew the FBI a map to my home. He was a former sniper, so he went into clear detail. Let this be a lesson. Your house is a show piece that demonstrates how faithfully you obey the law. It's a show piece to demonstrate your droning normality, your cognitive dissonance.

Now, For The Real Fun. Your Bug Out Locations

If you have the budget, I strongly encourage you to buy another house far away from yours, preferably one in the outskirts of town or farther. This provides you with a whole second house to go to, a second place to have stocked up with food, supplies, and community ties. Believe it or not, the gangs controlling your neighborhood can be a huge asset for your defense. Since you live there, you are a familiar face and therefore welcome. When shit hits the fan, they'll lock their area down and you'll be safe from almost any threat. It's this reason that you should be prepared to offer them either money or supplies for their services, just like tax dollars to our police. Yes, this is protection money but they're protecting you with hundreds of full auto weapons on their own turf. They can prove invaluable, just know who is who, what their personal motivation is, and what they expect in return. Every gang has good and bad cliques.

The pros of second, third, or more houses is that they're legal, you can hoard supplies into the walls to keep up appearances, you can have a second life set up in there, and it can be similar to a vacation home when decorated well. The cons are that you now have more taxes, which will be irrelevant in a government collapse, and you can be tracked through real estate records. All the more reason to obey every law.

Apartments are great in the city and a condo is even better. It gives you a location near work or an area close by for when you're in town. Whether drunk, shit hit the fan, or you're too tired to drive, a location in the city can be a huge asset to you. You can't do as much with the structural integrity of the place, but you can keep a fully stocked war closet for when you need it. Apartment buildings also offer more security than neighborhoods, especially in the city. Storefront cameras deter a lot of crime.

Cache Locations

These provide you with a smaller area where you can have supplies readily available to you. The cache location is a valuable asset in that you don't have to worry about a whole structure. You can simply bury a large, air/water-tight box with extra supplies. Personally, I keep a couple weeks of MREs, a single man tent, a ten-toot tarp, a Glock 19 with four magazines, five hundred feet of 550 cord, a compact space blanket sleeping bag, a change of clothing, boots, a Ka-Bar, and some first aid supplies. I crammed all that into a pair of 40 mm ammo cans.

Before burying your cache, research the area to know who owns it, how easily you can access it without being seen, and how easily you will be able to bury it . Woe to him who doesn't have a shovel when they need their supplies.

National forests and corporate lands are a great place to hide cache sites. Rarely does a police department or a business get installed in these and the area is generally owned or leased for a very long time. Make sure that your box is roughly four feet down to keep the temperature and humidity constant.

Dead Drops

If you don't have the funding for a second house, apartment, or a full cache site, a dead drop is a good solution. This is as simple as having an area close to you where you can put something without it being disturbed. If you're in an urban location and can't carry a firearm on you for whatever reason (perhaps you work in a courthouse or federal building) you may want to have a waterproofed pistol between work and your vehicle. Louisiana is a place with a lot of open areas, good forests, and plenty of hiding spots. I had a route that I normally went rucking on in my free time that was on post. Generally, you can't carry a firearm on a military installation, so I had dead drops along the way. In rural Louisiana, I could carry everywhere so I've never had any issues having several firearms on me.

For a dead drop location, it can be anywhere from a lock box, post office box, safe deposit box, or a small waterproof box hidden in a bush. The basics are always the same. Pistol, pocketknife, and a few hundred dollars. This way, if anything happens to your car, you can use your dead drop to get you through the stress.

Your Actual Bug Out Location

The area where you plan to run to in an emergency is your bug out location. Generally, a bug out location is similar to a hunting cabin that is far enough out in the woods to stay out of sight. It should be far enough out to not be seen on any common route and an area where passers-by will not stumble upon it. Research the area to make sure it's not a cross-country running zone or any other area where activities are hosted. The last thing you want to do is to find out that your bug out location is in the middle of a mountain bike racing route, cross-country run route, or where the local boy scouts do their land navigation.

One of the easiest bug out locations is a simple 20'x20' square cabin with a seven-foot ceiling. Regular 2"x4" studs for the walls, 2"x10" floor joists and rafters. Your roof should stand no higher than ten feet tall at the center. Your inner and outer walls are a simple 3/8" plywood. This, combined with high density foam insulation, will keep you happy all year. A wood stove can easily heat this structure and keep it hot even in the worst winters. Your supplies help insulate the walls and the structure is surprisingly strong. This type of encampment happily houses a small family and is small enough to keep out of sight. Your interior decoration ideas can vary from none at all to designing an elaborate castle. I recommend having two or three of these structures, with at least one being in another state.

If you want a more permanent location and have plenty of funds, consider building into a hillside or a mountain. Earth is your greatest armor. However, earth is extremely heavy. Two layers of sandbags will stop a mortar round but will snap a 2"x10" board when they get wet.

A marvel that I observed is a closed off culvert. Someone put a front and back door on a twenty-foot culvert. This created a great earth sheltered house that was waterproof. Granted, they had to dig a trench system for when it rained but it worked. The last thing you want to do though is live in a place that a planning commission decided to put a twenty-foot culvert due to the insane amount of water running through it. I recommend building your structure and simply burying it yourself. This way, you know how much weight is on it, how strong the root beds are on top of it, and where the water is going to go.

Steel shipping containers are another great asset. These strong yet cheap structures can be cut into any shape or size, joined, welded, and reinforced. Before playing with containers or steel construction at all, consult the professionals. Steel construction is effective but has very strict weight limits. By exceeding these limits, you guarantee your new structure is going to be a very expensive steel coffin.

No matter how you build your bug out location, you'll need to hide it. Your location should already be in a secure area that's not prone to flooding and be far enough from people to not be easily seen. Next, comes camouflage. There are no geometric shapes in nature, to include flat surfaces in nature. Greens, tans, grays, and browns are great spray paint colors that can help with hiding your shack. You highlight the deep areas with light colors and darken the high points. You should never have linear spray patterns or too much of one color in an area. Look at woodland camo patterns and you'll see a vast selection for reference. You can also use camouflage netting that's available from several retailers, just make sure that you dull it first. Then, comes your natural camouflage such as vines, grasses, trees, bushes, and other shrubs. Your windows will reflect shined light, so it pays to have dull, painted screens on the outside or use non-reflective veiling similar to what snipers use.

Once you're satisfied with your shack, it's time to put in natural defenses. Think of strategic areas to plant trees, thick shrubs, and bushes to hide your shack without limiting vital areas for you to view. Shortly beyond that, scatter seeds of all sorts of thorns, pickers, thistles, roses, brambles, mesquite trees, and whatever hellacious plants you wouldn't want to walk through. Go a couple hundred yards from your place to the hundred yard mark, you'll scatter as many seeds as you can. If the area is relatively untraveled by wildlife, you may consider actually planting the seeds. This forms a large defensive perimeter around your area that no one will pass through, unless they're coming to kill you.

Know Your Area

Walk all around the woods in your location and find out everything you can. The deer trails, high areas, low areas, water sources, can a fire tower see you? If you find yourself naturally taking a path, this is called a Natural Line of Drift. People and animals will follow these just as you have. Can you see your place form one of these? If so, thorns may need to be placed to keep things away. If you're an avid hunter, you may consider planting apple trees all over your yard so you can attract various animals. Animals can also help alert you to the presence of others. Your goal is to have people naturally drift away from your place while having friendly creatures around that will alert you to outsiders, such friends also become food in survival situations.

There are many back packers, explorers, and other folks who have nothing more to do in life than to explore the forest. These snoops are generally non-threatening, but you will want to keep them away from your area. Any one of those people can tell where your place is at and attract much unwanted attention. Very few of these people are willing to walk through thorny hell or bed down in those areas, so nature is your greatest defense.

In addition to walking around, you want to spend a few nights a month in areas within a mile of your cabin. This allows you to know the natural sounds of the area, get an idea of what wildlife is out there, and get a feel for the energy of your area. Around your cabin, be sure to urinate and defecate outside. This alerts animals of your presence and eliminates risk of surprising a predator.

If you're hunting, don't eat meat within a week of going out. The animals know when there's a predator around by the scent given off by carnivores. Prey can smell carnivores and generally avoid the area. You can also use this to your advantage. Eating a diet high in venison, red meat, and other animals will help secure your area from unwanted intrusions. Predators can smell predators and generally stay out of their turf. If not, you'll simply have to shoot and eat it.

What Should You Keep In A Bug Out Location?

The bug out location is where you keep your essential war supplies, your actual Bookshelf, and things to prepare for the worst. This is where your weapons, ammunition, combat boots, camouflage uniforms, ghillie suits, night vision, thermals, plate carrier, helmet, and war supplies are kept. Your Bookshelf is not just a regular bookshelf. This is where your war preparation books are kept. The law enforcement manuals, private investigations manuals, forensics books, body language, profiling, elicitation, counter-elicitation, surveillance, counter-surveillance, psychology, social psychology, sociology, survival books, emergency medicine, any texts regarding explosives or booby traps, cabin construction, living off the grid, deep woods hygiene, and productive leisure reading. Things to educate you and keep you sane while you're out there.

You'll also have to consider where to store wood for the wood stove, what kind of chain saw you want, and how to haul all this. You never want to cut down trees near your cabin as they help shield you. Go somewhere else entirely and get your wood there. Having a good pickup truck is great for this purpose. Use a sled to haul things easily. You probably already used a sled to get your wood stove to your cabin. It also pays to have plenty of mixed gas for your chain saw and a container or two of Bar & Chain oil. If you are ever out of Bar & Chain oil, any very dense oil will work.

As a wrap to chapter one, one thing is most important over all else. Preparation. Plans can go to shit in a heartbeat but being prepared for everything helps you roll with the punches, adapt to new problems, and have an idea of how to respond to emergencies. Instead of being caught off guard by an emergency, you're focused on the most effective solution that you've already rehearsed. Rehearsals are absolutely vital for every type of plan. Practice having you and your family bug out from different locations, make sure you have established meeting points, know how to get out of the area from several routes, prepare to be delayed, prepare to have to travel off road, prepare to have to defend yourself and your property. In times of chaos, there may be a riot on your planned route, protests across half the city, or a natural disaster that simply wrecks a road. I strongly advise reading every generic survival manual that you can get your hands on, so you have an idea of what right looks like.

As You Can Tell, This Is Not Going To Be Your Average Survival Book

This is intentionally disorganized to keep you thinking, I leave out key details so that you have to research and learn it yourself, and I pass you ideas for preparations that only you can fully develop. Giving you the answers, like most survival books do, is only useful when you can consult the text. By making you do your own research on certain subjects, you can control how in-depth you study, and you truly learn it. We learn by doing and we learn by teaching. I fully advise you to practice everything you learn in here, go over the scenarios with your family and friends (only those already preparing and are shown to be allies), and that you conduct regular rehearsals. Your imagination is your limit and builds adaptability, open mindedness, and helps you humor situations no matter how unrealistic. Plan for enemy invasions, earthquakes, zombies, the second coming of Christ, the nuclear war between the gods, solar flares, volcanoes, your neighbor's nuclear reactor melting down, the dam breaking, your boss hunting down you and your family, orangutan hordes in the streets, wild viral outbreaks, gas attacks, wildfires, kamikaze satellites, and whatever else you can think of. Nothing is impossible. The last thing you want is to find out that the forest fire really was started by rabid lab hamsters who took control of a space station and are using its solar panels as a giant magnifying glass.

Preparedness Helps In Mysterious Ways

I had a friend in prison who was doing twenty years for a manslaughter case. His girlfriend died of a stab wound and she bled out before he could get her to the hospital. Had he known the second use for a tampon, she would still be alive, and he wouldn't be doing the rest of his life in prison. Things like this can make all the difference in life. Or death for that matter.

By being prepared, you can be that everyday hero that makes a huge difference in someone's life. I've been a first responder to a fatal motorcycle-deer collision on LA 28, stopped a suicide attempt, and happened upon several motor vehicle collisions. I approach these situations calmly and collectedly because I know how to perform trauma treatment, assess dangers on scene, and keep situations cool. Everyone is capable of doing this, they just have to know what to do beforehand. I preach preparedness day in and day out. It can be the only difference between life and death. Not only for others but also for you, your family, and those you care about.

Chapter 2

Defending Proactively

Once Again, I Stress Education More Than Anything

The more educated you are, the more able you are to see your options when it comes time to defend our life and property. Chess players are good at the game because they know more battle strategies and react to the board. You must know the angles your enemy is going to hit, what your weaknesses are, and think two steps ahead of them. The more thoroughly you look into things, the more details you will notice. Success and failure both are determined by the details. Once you know something well, practice it non-stop until it becomes a habit. Most people practice until they can get it right, the successful practice until they can't get it wrong. This is the mentality that you need to be in. Study everything on the Bookshelf and then some. Become adept in carpentry, soldering, welding, small engine repair, residential wiring, electric logic, gunsmithing, blade smithing, glass blowing, residential plumbing, sewing by hand and machine, sheet metal work, automotive design and repair, and whatever you think will stump you in the future. Your efforts to expand your mind and skills must be constant. If you do this, you'll be able to fix most of life's problems. You'll be able to work on everything around the house, repair your own things, and even get into business doing these services for others. Don't just be the jack of all trades, be the mantle of knowledge.

Your situational awareness is your greatest asset. With all of these skills, you'll see through the eyes of a cop, master criminal, engineer, carpenter, repairman, tailor, and whatever other trades you've picked up. With skill, even life's hardest problems become simple.

Quite simply, if you don't know what to look for, you'll miss everything. You cannot prepare for a threat that you cannot see so it pays to have the broadest knowledge base that you can. This knowledge base is the foundation for every future skill and encounter. Federal Agents train relentlessly to discover new threats before they arise and so should you. By proactively seeking these problems out, you reduce the chance of surprise when it matters the most. One of the problems is that the feds don't get the play time that they need to truly become adept and routinely make mistakes.

In my chemical weapons case, even veteran federal agents overlooked vital details and made critical mistakes. They, as veteran federal agents, have a lot to learn which means that you have even more.

Knowing The Enemy Is Hard

Look at all of the police agencies near you, the sheriff's deputies, the state police, FBI, ATF, United States Marshals, DEA, Customs and Border Protection, the Forest Service, the Game Warden, and even the military. Everything they wear is available online, which is often their main source for after-market gear which they routinely use. This breaks up the uniformity and adds individualism to each agent or officer. Criminals use this to their advantage when impersonating law enforcement. Official vehicles are nothing more than performance enhanced vehicles with lights and a siren system. Their performance chips are far outclassed by what is available online, their lights are cheap and readily available online, and even their siren systems are common. Their radios are easy to get, it all boils down to programming the right frequencies into a radio with the police band. Even their specialized gear to include the thermals and night vision, short barrel rifles, short barrel shotguns, tasers, suppressors, ballistic vests, breaching tools, hand cuffs, zip cuffs, hand cuff keys, cuff cutters, expandable batons, OC spray, tear gas, smoke grenades, and even flash-bang grenades. It's available online and surprisingly cheap.

The enemy may, and does, portray professionalism, have rank structure, and impersonate law enforcement to sow confusion. Across the nation, criminals have used police equipment to rob rival gangs and drug dealers. When robbing drug dealers, they often set up "controlled buys" where they have other dealers or customers meet them, where they too are robbed. The only problem with this is that they frequently make mistakes, disregard key parts of law, break procedures that only real police know, lack confidence, and lack the matter-of-fact attitude possessed by real cops.

Working alongside of two military police companies, Customs and Board Protection's BMTF, several local police departments, and countless months of study, training, and practice have shown me what right looks like. It's shown me the good cops, the bad cops, the lazy cops, and the extremely switched on cops, but none-the-less they're all real cops serving under lawful authority. I've learned the lingo, the demeanor, and the actions of real cops under stress.

The other end of the spectrum are the highly trained individuals posing as street criminals. This phenomenon is when special operations personnel, SWAT officers, experienced detectives or combat veterans pose as

Who's real?

street criminals to rob banks, take out drug houses for personal profit, destroy their own evidence, or anything else they set their mind to. Many officers, regardless of agency, will pocket valuable evidence. It's important to know the difference between the two groups. One will use lawful authority to victimize you where the other will portray lawful authority so you can shoot them. A criminal posing as a cop may not even have armor plates in his vest, have a non-working radio, and react poorly to lawful challenges to their procedures. They might even be toting around a concealed carry permit badge instead of a counterfeit one. Those small differences can be all it takes from switching our mentality to gathering a badge number in order to file a complaint against the officer, to realizing that he's a fake and you're about to be robbed. I recommend robbing anyone dumb enough to pose as law enforcement. By rob, I clearly mean, "hold them under citizen's arrest until law enforcement can take custody and bring him before a court of law."

The next step in knowing your enemy is to learn your area. Most gang turf is controlled by small cliques and the members know each other. Should you have an issue with them, you may be able to talk to their "big homie" and remedy the wrong before going to drastic measures. In order to do this though, you have to have earned their respect.

It's also important to know who is in control of the area and what kind of gang they are. Are they racial supremacists, political extremists, or a band of hoodlums? Take note of their gang's colors, their numbers, their vehicles, their residences, what kind of weapons they carry, the respect level, primary sources of income, and how fast they can reinforce. Should they be decent people who are more of an armed yet unlawful neighborhood watch, you may be able to use them as security assets or as a distraction.

It pays to know when a dude who you believe holds his pistol sideways may begin spraying rounds out of a machine pistol. At that point, anything in front of him is going to be in serious trouble. Many of the gang shootings involve stray bullets to innocent bystanders. Learn what triggers these people, their weapons capabilities, and overall intelligence level. You will automatically know that if they only carry pistols, you can safely engage them from slightly beyond pistol range. Depending on their skill level, you may be able to engage them from well within pistol range. There are also several new gang members who only want to spray a few rounds to prove that they have the balls to use a gun. More often than not, they hit nothing or fire into the air. I was locked up with a dude who ended up in the feds for accidently firing his pistol while slapping someone with it during a home invasion.

The few street members who do tote long guns will rarely have a good supply of ammunition, so their capability is severely limited. You'll also rarely see street shootings last more than a minute. Once the rounds are fired, gunshot sensors automatically notify police of a shooting and the participants are already running from the scene, regardless of whether or not they hit their target. Some are already running away by the time the shooting begins, this is why you see them with a pistol firing wildly behind them as they flee. Most gang shooters want to ditch their firearm as soon as possible so as not to be caught with it.

The main problem with gangs it that their numbers provide a false sense of security. They act out, flex their numbers, and expect everyone to bow. They generally reinforce quickly, and some may even wish to shoot at the arriving police before running off. This gives them more street credit and also antagonizes responding officers to respond by returning fire, often to suppress the threat long enough to maneuver on it.

You will rarely have to get into a gunfight with gangs. Most of them have a criminal record that prohibits them from owning a firearm. Simply get a good surveillance camera and take good photos of them with firearms. Send those photos to the police and the prosecutor and you'll see half of their numbers end up in federal prison.

Should you ever have to take on a gang, take longer distance shots with an accurate rifle. Use a suppressor to avoid setting off gunshot sensors and hit them in a pattern. Hit their small groups with rapid, accurate shots and engage the reinforcements from a covered location. Always have a way out. Once word gets out that there's action on a block, you can lie in wait for them at their houses or raid the other streets while they're distracted. Once you get a few threats eliminated, leave rival gang colors at the scene or tag their turf to leave a calling card. The more of each other they kill, the less you'll have to worry about.

Counter-elicitation

Whether your adversary is a lawful interrogator or a street thug screening you for entry into a crew, their job is going to be to harvest information from you. Seemingly simple questions can have drastic consequences for others or yourself down the road. Elicitation itself is a method of getting a targeted person to divulge critical information.

They generally establish a base line for how you respond, your body language, time it takes you to answer, how your eyes move, changes in tics, and how evenly you answer questions. They'll try to establish a rapport with you and assure that you're comfortable. They can take advantage of your natural need to correct an error by tossing in a bogus detail. They will use sympathy, empathy, mirror your body language, flatter you, and act as if they can justify your actions. Then, they go way deeper. They want to know what time of day it was, what the weather was like, what you ate that day, the clothes you were wearing, what you drank that day, how high the sidewalk curbs are, what shade the roads were, what the pattern of gunfire sounded like, what the light poles are made of, whether or not there's lines on the street, what color houses are, did the offenders reload, how many people shot, who shot at who, what were they yelling, whether or not they were pistol or rifle shots, what each person was wearing, why you were there in the first place, how many cars were present, what kind of cars, and the list can go on. Their intention is to have you give more information than the average liar can remember giving, get you to slip up, get nervous at certain questions, and get to the truth. Remember that it's all a game. By maintaining a calm, glib demeanor, you can shut down their efforts unless they're a trained professional. Should you ever be up against a trained professional, try to avoid the interview altogether. If you ever have to talk with a trained professional, tell the whole truth and nothing but the truth. Even when you do this, they'll still try to catch you up in things even if they can clearly verify your story. If you want to catch a mouse, make a noise like a cheese. . .

Counter-surveillance

If you're being watched, you have two options. To learn their methods to defeat them or have fun with them. When on camera, be on camera. Be the innocent, hard-working person that you are no matter what. All they can report on is what they personally observe of you. If you want to play, start wearing a rabbit or dog costume around your house as if this is normal, tan on your roof at night, mop your lawn in the rain, mow your driveway, ride the mailbox like a horse, take a nap under the car, build an alter to the Marshmallow God on your front lawn and pray to the holy s'more. Things like this will make it hard for them to concentrate, wonder what you're really up to and let them know that their surveillance is blown. If you want to play with them, several neat toys are available online. If you suspect that they're using a shotgun-mic to listen in on you or another means such as precision laser audio surveillance, put your nods (night vision optical devices) on and take a look around. The laser will paint a straight line to the operator. White-noise generators are also very useful in certain applications to block out parabolic-mic capabilities. By putting infrared (IR) lights around your outer perimeter, you can blind anyone who has nods without disturbing the neighbors. If it's dark, they can't see. When their nods are flared, they can't see. If they're using Thermal IR technology, the thermals can't see through glass. Regular glass reflects the ability to monitor temperature changes behind it and will appear as either solid black or solid white though thermals. You can flare their nods with IR lights, have them switch to thermals and simply watch them from your window and they won't be able to see you. As it's dark, their natural night vision may kick in so have a backup. Personally, I trust ultra-bright LED strips to accomplish this. By pulsing them every thirty seconds in three second bursts, you guarantee that they are unable to see anything.

Next, we get into lens finders. These emit a huge wave of lasers that refract and glow when they hit the convex shape of a camera lens. This works even on pen sized cameras. They're commonly used in addition to Radio Frequency (RF) finders while doing counter-surveillance sweeps of rooms that will hold important meetings. RF finders can be effective only if you control the place and guarantee that the only electronics there are contraband. This involves having no other electronics nearby for any reason. RF finders will detect everything, sometimes they'll even trigger for the electric lines in the wall. One of the best ideas to take out a surveillance crew is to simply call the police and report a peeping Tom. The responding officers will make contact with the team which will show you how many personnel you're dealing with. If the police allow them to stay, they're conducting lawful surveillance. If they're not doing lawful surveillance, they're going to be arrested.

If you're being followed by a surveillance team, you may be in for a show. These mobile teams generally employ many operators that continuously box you in as you move. They have street walkers that linger in a perimeter for two blocks in all directions of you and multiple vehicles will often be driving ahead of you, parallel to you, and two vehicles will be behind you. Let's talk behind you, the first car is their lead car, and they will drive in a normal manner, generally two vehicles behind you or in the other lane. They will not slow down or assure that they follow you. Should you suddenly stop, slow down, or turn around, they will keep going. The next vehicle behind them will take over as the lead vehicle. If you stop, both vehicles will keep going and a foot operator will soon take over. A trail vehicle may even turn a corner, let out their passenger, and wait elsewhere. If you're on foot, never round three sides of the box. Basically, don't make two consecutive left or right turns. You may end up walking right up to their main staging point and then you're in a very bad position.

Your surveillance crew will also never be all pairs of slightly hidden men. This is universally known as a troublesome sign. They'll often pair up with females, pose as couples, and rarely do they care about being seen. They become pedestrians of their environment, posing as shoppers, travelers, store employees and others in traffic. A good tail is never truly lost, only played with. Things such as sudden stops, changes in directions, U-turns from a parking spot, and changing routes are common techniques that are planned for in surveillance operations. You may lose one, or even four of the operators, but you'll never be truly free. If you demonstrate that you're a hard target, it's generally accepted that you are trained and have something serious to hide. You'll either get them to deploy GPS, drones, or more thorough surveillance methods. The downside of this is that if you truly spook them, they may just eliminate you as a valid threat. You've heard the conspiracy theories that people get "disappeared" and are stuck under a "too dangerous to release" category, are held indefinitely under the PATRIOT act, or simply end up garroted. I'm not saying that these claims have any merit, but people do disappear for various reasons at the hand of government, street organizations, and the mob on a regular basis. More often than not, these paid job handlers do not work for any specific organization and exercise impunity from any problems.

Let's Face Reality Here

We are in the modern day surveillance age. No matter where we go, there's cameras in businesses, multiple cameras on our phones, voice recognition, facial recognition, gait recognition, pattern recognition, cameras front and back on everyone's lap top computers, then there's the drones . . . there's really no reason anymore to have a surveillance team. You can be followed 24/7 without a break without someone having to leave their recliner. Everything you do, say, or browse is being monitored.

Acquiring Assets

If society collapses, lawlessness will abound. You may now be able to get your hands on things that you were previously unable to even lay eyes on. During times of looting, chaos, and insanity, anything can happen to include mass robberies. Use this to your advantage. Join the unarmed looters in places you know have weak security. I'm sure you noticed in the nationwide protests of 2019-2022 that anything goes. Police vehicles were set on fire, court houses were firebombed, city blocks were taken over, and the national guard was widely used to intervene. However, our military, even under the authority of martial law, will rarely harm our citizens unless absolutely necessary. The people truly control the nation and can quickly seize control at any time. This leaves many regimes, extremist groups, religious groups, and other political affiliates waiting to gain power. Each of these have lawful, valid ideals and also a nefarious side. It's important to know who is who, what their goals are, and whether or not moving into another district will protect you. At the first sign that an enemy group is coming into power, it's time to strike.

Get your hands on as much of their equipment as possible and learn it fluently. Get their radios so you have their communications but beware of a GPS function. Their weapons are best to use since each one of them will have ammunition for them. Get a hold of their vehicles. Learn how to use them, how to get into them during combat, know to destroy them, and where the major security flaws are. Learn what the drivers and occupants can see from their point of view and what methods they have to use to egress from the vehicle. For most armored vehicles, they have two doors and a rear hatch. Being welded in prohibits their exit. The combat locks on the doors can be manipulated with a wrench from the outside. Their ballistic windows are useless when spidered. The windshield on our old vehicles weighed close to three hundred pounds each and were set in at an angle. When spidered, these windows cannot simply be kicked out. The vehicle is blind where it sits. If you are able to take one out, beware. You only have a few seconds to gather as much as you can before their reinforcements arrive. Once shooting starts, they've already notified their higher element that they have an element in contact and a force is quicky coming to help them. If you disabled the vehicle, leave it. If not, steal it. Just beware of GPS systems that you would never think to look for. This is a huge reason to have a team. Should you be successful, you can only carry so much, and you can only drive one vehicle. You can never have too much help carrying things, especially when it comes down to a foreign military takeover involving armored vehicles, a gang takeover where they've gained police armored vehicles, or any other nation-wide emergency.

If your enemy is too high in number or hitting them directly isn't an option, take out their supply lines. It's then time to ghillie up and be a guerilla. Sabotage, espionage, and subterfuge are great assets. Steal what you can and destroy the rest. Never, ever try to hit the same location twice. By doing this, you'll end up running into the new security detail or find out the hard way that they placed a sniper to watch the site. Take what you can the first time and leave nothing behind for them

It's important in these times to network people. The more like-minded people you are in contact with, the more places you have to stash items, spread out vital supplies, each person is a new pair of eyes and ears, they can assist in raids, and you have multiple places to stay while you're out operating.

Enjoy The Home, House And Bunker

No matter where you're at, if you have your family and friends, you're at home. It pays to enjoy the place as long as it doesn't jeopardize operation security. Obviously no disco parties, RAVEs, or keggers in your bug out locations or where you plan to survive at. For the home, bug out locations, and bunker, it pays to have nice carpet, plants or fake plants, good furniture, good heat, and good air conditioning.

In the home, have some salt candles burning, some incense, scented candles, have a lava lamp or one of those exotic electric balls that follow you when you touch it. Those items make the place feel better, add distractions, and can put you at ease in stressful situations. Lighting certain rooms with Christmas lights, having nice artwork, and collecting items give your home a good appearance and can add to the calm in certain rooms. For the bunker, you can paint scenes of Paris, Rome, Sparta, Dubai, or anywhere else you want onto the wall. Or, you can get a giant photo of it printed out. Put up a window frame and curtains to make it look as if you are gazing out your patio into these beautiful lands. Add a lamp behind the curtain rod to simulate letting the sun in and small fans on each side to simulate a breeze coming in. You can create these scenes differently for every room of the house. Perhaps the kitchen window above the sink is a scene of Iowa. Not a worry in the world, just watching the corn grow as you wash dishes. See how cool that could be?

Even in Afghanistan, I'd hang Christmas lights around my plywood room, I'd have my favorite music playing, a candle burning, and I always had my decorative Hookah readily available for smoking. The many flavors of Shisha create excellent smoke rings, help you relax, and make it seem as if you aren't living in hell.

Have Indoor Plants

Not just plants but also vegetables. High Pressure Sodium (HPS) lights replicate sunlight and the full UV spectrum for plants to grow healthy. I learned this from people who used to grow hundreds of marijuana plants in their homes. As long as you have good soil in a large pot, know how to fertilize properly, have a good water source, and proper light cycles, you can grow almost anything indoors. Your favorite flowers, tomatoes, apple tree saplings, all sorts of peppers and spices, will all grow happily. Just beware that they, too, breathe oxygen at night. In prison, I grow apple trees, tomatoes, an onion, a potato, grass, and clovers. All I use is natural light from the window, a soda box full of dirt, and sink water. My plants grow slowly but they're doing great. I know what you're thinking, grass? Yes, grass. Every man needs to practice good lawn care habits no matter where he's at.

Pets Are A Great Addition

Hamsters, rabbits, mice, rats, guinea pigs, chinchillas, gerbils, and birds are great. They're small, kept in enclosures, and storing their food doubles as insulation until it's needed. Birds can get loud so always consider the circumstances you keep it in. The HPS light provide the same effect of sunlight to you and the animals, but these can get very hot so beware of overheating the place.

Just Because The Whole Earth Has Gone Into Crisis, Does Not Mean That You Have To Live Poorly.

Cook good food and enjoy it. The MREs are always to be a last resort. You should even consider hunting for food. Only when you're entirely out of food should you ever eat an MRE. The same goes for your survival preps. They are exactly that, survival preps and are your last known food supply. Only use them if you're going to die. You have the means to grow, hunt, and barter so you should never have to use your own supplies.

Comfortable Living

Scented trash bags, cotton swabs, tweezers, scissors, floss, fresh toothbrushes, metal can openers, board games, video games, movies, and razors are game changers.

Staying happy and healthy in survival situations is the key to getting through it. Those simple things are luxuries when everyone else is struggling to eat and keep warm. Consider Epsom salt, hot water bottles, cooking supplies, the spices you enjoy, moleskin for foot problems, freezer packs, eucalyptus oil, aloe, menthol oil, tea tree oil, things like this make all the difference and are natural remedies. Consider also that the worst thing in the world is a toothache. Always have a full set of dental tools, anesthetic, crown cement, temporary filling material, and PLENTY of salt. Sodium Chloride works miracles in life. Keep Pounds of it. These simple things mean the difference between life and death in some cases.

Take time right now and look through Maslow's Hierarchy of Needs and several similar ideas. If your needs aren't being met, you simply won't survive, you damn sure won't thrive, and you surely will not advance at anything you attempt. I'll close out chapter two with a piece of good advice to you.

Admit Nothing, Deny Everything, and Trust No One

Teams work well when everyone's goals are aligned but all it takes is one single moment of strife to turn a friend to an enemy. Even if there was no wrong done, their perception of a wrong is all it takes. Whether they feel shorted in a deal, unequally worked, or are simply having a bad day, things can quickly change. This person is, from that point on, dangerous to you and your organization. Everything they know, they will speak on or use to exploit you. At their chosen moment of opportunity, they will burn you and leave you wondering what happened as you're trying to clean up a giant mess.

No organization is free from traitors. Criminal organizations have Rats, federal organizations have criminals, social organizations have dissenters, extremist groups have mediators, and even the peace groups have extremists. No matter how strict you maintain accountability, they always have an opportunity to betray you. If you show no trust and take all of their ability to betray you away, they quickly become disloyal, and the hatred begins to grow. This is why every member of your group has to already have their own plans, assets, and values already in place. Time is the only determinant of dedication, but that dedication can quickly fade. Simple disagreements even over whether to execute captured enemies can quickly divide a group. Both sides are like-minded, good people but things like this can turn them into enemies.

If these types of people are captured by a like-minded enemy or simply interviewed by a skilled elicitor, everything they know will quickly fall into the hands of their captors. Ask any drug dealer, they'll quickly tell you that they've done prison time for a customer that ratted on them, but they won't tell you who they ratted on to get time off their sentence. Anything and everything can change someone's mind when things go wrong.

I'm confident that you now know the limitless scum-baggery that the world contains, and I know you've learned a few tricks to live happily when things go wrong.

The next part of this book will get directly into the actions you need to take when things go wrong, how to build up defenses, and put reality into perspective. As you're thrown into a world where everyone is now a potential enemy, you'll either follow this advice or die wishing you had. Ever hear the phrase "I'd rather have my gun and not need it than to need it and not have it?" Well, this is your gun. Depending on what happens in the world around you, this gun may only have one bullet. Your one final chance to get out alive and continue to see your family alive. When shit hits the fan, chaos will prevail and only those in the know will make it out. The difference between street smart and formal education will quickly be known to all.

Chapter 3

Surviving The Beginning

No matter how skilled of a craftsman, blacksmith, carpenter, welder, bladesmith, gunsmith, architect, nurse, police officer, soldier, or whatever else you may be good at, you're not good enough. When things go bad, all of your skills will be put to the absolute test. You will be pushed to your absolute limits and even to the breaking point. Life as you know it will be drastically changed, materials will not be as easily available, and you may be severely outnumbered by an armed enemy. Your permanent residence and any locations near you may be completely compromised by rioters, looters, and anyone who knows you have supplies. This leaves you with two options. 1) Run like hell; or 2) prepare to hunker down and defend your property.

Should you choose option 2, you'd better have all of your affairs in order and one hell of a disaster-proof structure waiting to receive you. If not, you'll have to build one. If you're going to build one, I suggest that you begin blueprinting with this chapter in mind. If you already have a good shelter, use this chapter to add new ideas and tricks to the party.

Whether you're building new, or you've chosen to turn your home into a bunker, it's important to thoroughly know your area. You need to know the sounds of your place. The doors that squeak, the floors that grumble, the stairs that whine, and the boards that howl. Just as in nature, only humans will make certain sounds. If you pay attention, you can identify which of your family members are walking around based on their steps, the shoes they wear, and their pace.

Personally, I knew the sounds of everyone in my platoon as they walked down the hallway. During my first deployment, we were out in Torkham which is a village divided by the Khyber Pass of Afghanistan. Half the village is in Afghanistan and the other half is in Pakistan. We had the luxury of an actual building to sleep in which had solid floors. Based on the footsteps coming down the hall, I knew when my roommate was about to be back, when it was a squad leader coming through, and when the First Sergeant was doing his rounds. You will be able to do this with just a bit of attention to detail. You'll also be able to tell which of your pets is on the move based on their steps.

These types of noises can let you know that whoever is moving around your home, they're not someone that belongs. This can be a determinant of whether or not to fire through a dummy wall or dump a burst down the hall.

As you see, we've come upon the subject of **Dummy Wall**. This is a wall that is not reinforced, not structural, and may be placed anywhere simply to divert foot traffic into your traps. A **Dummy Wall** is a regularly constructed wall that you keep hollow to allow rounds to penetrate, having maximum effect on an intruder. Your dummy wall will normally be covered with drywall on the side visible to others. It's much cheaper this way.

If you're not sure what the Fatal Funnel is, look it up. You can use dummy walls to create a fake foyer on your main door that continues for ten feet to extend your fatal funnel, or you could have the dummy wall direct intruders to one corner of a room. A simple trip wire near the end that's attached to a bell will let you know when to spray the whole wall with rounds. If you chose the hallway method of extending your fatal funnel, you can pie the corner after the breach was made. You'll have them trapped in an inescapable hell tunnel. You can get creative with this too. Instead of a dummy wall, you can use reinforced walls to achieve the same thing, only this time you'll be safe to detonate a claymore in the hall without causing damage to the rest of your home. You can do half walls which are only at waist height so they will have to cross over it, leading them to a bear trap, or simply slowing them down enough to break their T or strong-wall formation. You can also put another dummy wall at the end, so they're boxed in. There's nothing like having a good breach that only leads to a maze-like dead end. It's essentially a meat grinder that guarantees your failure.

Reinforced Construction and Armoring

Several easy steps can make all the difference in defending your place. When your home comes under direct fire, bullets will rip through walls, tumble, mushroom out, create spalling, and destroy whatever is in their path. Big rounds will blow your chest out your back, medium rounds expand and tumble through you, and small rounds tend to bounce around inside you like a pinball. The cheapest way to overcome this threat is to line your outer walls. As a sheet of plywood is 4'x8', you can make a ballistic sandwich. The **Ballistic Sandwich** is a sheet of 3/4'" plywood sandwiched between two 1/8" pieces of sheet steel. You bolt these all together at each corner and at the half-way points. You screw these into the studs of your outside walls as needed and they'll create a four foot

high bullet barrier for you. Instead of drywall, you make a bunch of these sandwiches and hang those. You can drywall the outside and your place looks just the same. Wallpaper, decorate, hang art, just know that you won't be able to screw anything into the actual wall anymore. If you still want to be able to hang things, you'll have to pre-drill holes through the inner steel and remember not to drive your screws through to the other side.

Most rounds will be stopped by the Ballistic Sandwich. The outer steel will mushroom the round and the plywood will stop the spalling. However, some hard rounds will punch through one sheet and normally get stopped by the other. There are specialty rounds such as armor-piercing rounds, sabot light armor penetrating, and armor-piercing incendiary which will rip through quite a bit more than what you have. Also, nearly nothing can stop a .50 BMG round from hitting its mark. The regular full metal jacket in that caliber will wreck your walls. There's specialty rounds that are designed to take out armored vehicles that will chew through your defenses with ease. Almost nothing will survive the Ma Deuce .50 so if you're being engaged by one, running is your best option. Unless you have a custom built house with a brick exterior with an interior Ballistic Sandwich of half inch steel, one inch plywood, and another half inch steel. However, this is insanely heavy, and very expensive. It still will not stop a .50 SLAP or .50 API round, let alone at the rate the Ma Deuce can sling them.

If you prefer not to have to change the outer wall structure of your home, consider a safe room. You can re-do the structural work for one room of your house and use your choice of Ballistic Sandwich for each wall, ceiling, and floor.

This creates a problem though, **ventilation**. If you can't breathe you're dead and quite simply, that much armor in a room does not allow air flow. This means that you'll have to have a dedicated intake and exhaust system in order to breathe. This can be expensive and can also compromise your entire operation. If the intake gets filled with smoke, gas, or is deliberately blocked by your enemy, you will slowly die. It is absolutely vital that you have a good ventilation system, hide its intake and exhaust vents, and that the enemy cannot find them even through a dedicated search. To get you out of a safe room, your enemy may burn the house down around you, try to gas you out, cut through your walls with a torch, flood you out, or combine their methods by pumping diesel fuel into your intake vent. Personally, I'd just block your door or weld it shut then rob you blind. But, it's all about their motivation. A single Molotov Cocktail can turn your box into an oven. Remember that.

It is also vital to hide your door. I suggest a very small door, something that no one would suspect. Many safe room doors are behind bookshelves which can be obvious to a threat. I recommend having your safe room covered by your bathroom medicine cabinet, a single panel between the shelves of your pantry, or a narrow passage through the floor. Your options are your imagination so get creative.

If you are also not into safe rooms, perhaps a single room of your house such as a walk-in closet will suffice. Reinforce the wall, put on a strong door frame, and install a thick door.

If you want to go all out, build a custom front wall. By replacing your exterior walls' 2"x4" studs with 2"x12" studs, you create the foundation to use full 12"x12" post, I call them trunks, as a door frame. This allows you to rabbet the inner piece to have a three-inch gap into them. With a hell of a Door Sandwich such as an inch of solid oak, 1/4 inch steel, three-quarter inch flat plywood and another inch of oak sandwiched together, you've got one hell of a door that will sit flush with the frame. This allows you to get creative with deadbolts and all sorts of locks. Just be sure that your extra locks are not visible from the outside. The extra key holes are a big sign saying, "shoot breaching round here."

Regardless of how you use this type of wall construction, it comes in handy. So, now that you have a few rounds in the magazine to employ to your benefit, it's important that you can see what the enemy is doing and when they leave. **This brings us to surveillance cameras**. Your cameras are your situational awareness asset and without them, you are stuck playing the "what if?" game. When installing cameras, make sure that the cameras themselves are not visible and all of your wiring is neatly hidden. The first thing a competent enemy will do is hit your house from every angle using a lens finder then try to trace the cameras to the power source, establish where the data storage is, and locate their field of view. For this reason, you should always veil your cameras. Regular veiling or even a piece of screen work really well and defeat most lens finders. Get online and purchase dummy cameras and stick them all over the place. This will deter most criminals who believe they're on camera from coming around. This will also sow confusion in your enemies as they'll be trying to find out the usual information on cameras that are not actually connected.

Once you have this in place, it's time to think. Think to yourself, "What would stop me from coming into my house?" "How would I break into my house?" "How would I get in if I had a team to coordinate with?" "How would we get in if we had a vehicle?" The most common answers are all the weak spots. The doors or door frames, the windows, the roof, the walls, the floors, or to simply flush the occupants out. Simple things can deter all efforts. A team is useless once the hounds are released. Vehicles rarely do good when the walls are reinforced and tied together with reinforcement bar. Your creativity is your absolute limit so get creative.

This part of the planning phase is just like playing chess with yourself. Think of everything you would do and then think of the worst case scenario. Harden your weak spots, provide false weak spots that are actually traps, use fake doors, use fake windows, use all sorts of tools that are available in hardware stores to play hell with your enemy. Always remember, if you have to fire a live round, you're already stressing too much.

The greatest defense against an enemy is to plan for their actions beforehand and to see them first. If they don't have the element of surprise and you expect what they'll do, you can use this all against them. There is zero limit to the amount of hell you can create, especially if you're good with robotics. You need not even be in the home to terrorize an invading enemy. How you handle yourself in these situations is a direct reflection of whether or not you live or die. Sometimes the pre-combat beers are necessary to keep your nerves steady, especially if you're the one being hunted.

Notice them first. The more surveillance cameras, early warning devices, and security assets you have for your home, the better off you'll be no matter what you're up against. We're now going to dig far deeper into what you can do to notice the enemy while they're on approach.

I've spent thousands of hours posted in static security positions overseas and hundreds at similar positions in the US. There's simply things that you pick up by staying alert in those situations that prove invaluable, things that most people will never notice in life. I've been both on the attack and on the defense in Afghanistan, been through the Joint Readiness Training Center at Fort Polk on several rotations and had the privilege of doing several OPFOR (opposing forces) rotations with the 509th Airborne Infantry. Many people do not know the skills that the 509th has to offer and they'll never hear of the absolutely priceless training that they provide for our Nation's forces.

The JRTC at Fort Polk is the final meat grinder that deploying Army units will endure before they go on a combat deployment. The 509th exploit every weakness, monopolize on the smallest inattention to detail, and are the final gut check delivered to entire brigades before they're tested in ground combat overseas. Rarely will a rotation unit succeed against the 509th and it's commonplace for platoon sized elements to take out several companies in a single night. The tactics used create a personal hell for the rotational unit and fully demonstrate the seriousness of the reality they face. Now, enough swinging on the 509th's nuts. Check them out online and you'll see the wild and amazing things they do.

In addition to great training, I've had the privilege of serving alongside the 19th Special Forces Group in Kandahar and Helmand provinces of Afghanistan. The second-half of my second deployment was spent alongside the 7th Special Forces Group far north in Kabul. They refined the foundation of knowledge that I'd amassed and ironed out all the major wrinkles for our company.

Through enduring several rotations against the 509th and several rotations alongside them, I've picked up pieces of information that will allow you to ruin your enemy as they approach and finish them off while they're on your lawn. Should they ever get to your building, they won't get into it and surely they'll find surprises on the inside. The following are products of years of experience, absolute hell, and absolutely great minds.

The First Thing We'll Discuss Is Out of Focus Nods

To properly focus nods, you first make sure your depth perception is equal to your non enhanced eye, then you focus them in on a star in the night sky. This makes a huge difference. Some clowns have their nods to where it looks like they're looking backward through binoculars (field glasses.) Others have them focused in too near to where the objects in the distance are fuzz. Some have them focused too far out and everything near them is fuzz which causes them to trip, stumble, fall, and make noise.

Once you get the focus correct, **on a star**, make sure the things are not too far away from your face. The nods shine a green light that will light up your face as if you were a glowing ogre creeping through the woods. We'd see this kind of thing constantly with rotational units and it gives away their positions.

Next, We Have Earpieces For Radios

Yes, they're absolutely handy because you can receive instructions without anyone else around you being able to hear anything. However, you still have to talk into your hand mic which can give away your position. The greatest flaw with the earpieces though is that the earpiece becomes an earplug while not in use. This severely limits the enemy's situational awareness, and you wouldn't believe how easily you can walk right up to them. When under fire, the earpiece is useless and blocks out no sound. Leaving you deaf in one ear and unable to hear instructions at all. This also contributes to hearing loss in the long run. Round after round, explosion after explosion, all unguarded by the little plastic earpiece.

But, Beware

Commercially available items such as Peltor muffs and a new thing called the TCAPS can link directly into two radios, and they offer ambient sound amplifications while blocking out gunshots. With the volume all the way up on the ambient sound, you can hear your fingers click together, your breathing sounds like a horror film phone call and you can whisper to your buddies at a hundred meters. These muffs and TCAPS earbuds do the exact same thing. They greatly amplify ambient sound, allow perfect radio communication, and completely block gunshot or explosion frequencies from being heard. All you feel is the pressure of the shot. You can get a cheap pair of these for roughly $40 online and they work great but have no radio capability. The real Peltors and TCAPS will run you several thousands of dollars depending on what you need them for. I began using them in training because my deaf ass used to be point man on several operations. My squad leader, roughly 20 meters back would have to resort to tossing rocks at me to get my attention. These wonder-muffs solved all of my problems. In my free time, my team completely quit using radios. We'd simply wear our wonder-muffs to have whisper conversations across the buildings to each other or even from building to building on a calm night.

Next, We Get Into Radios and Why They Suck

Depending on the type of radio you're using, some may broadcast static at inopportune times, some have a battery chirp function, and some chirp after each transmission or to let you know that your keyed up on the net. Another issue is the hot-mic, which is where someone is accidentally leaning on their push to talk and is now broadcasting everything they say to everyone on that particular frequency. It's a pain in the ass, especially when you're trying to sneak into a building while having to hear potato chips crunching or worse.

In the Khyber pass, we had a dude hot-mic on the company net while having an in depth conversation on how our commander is a piece of shit. That's one way that radios can backfire on you.

Also in the Khyber pass, we had these new radios which had no screens. Everything was pre-loaded by a computer and would give you verbal feedback of your channel, volume level and battery level. These things gave a battery alert at certain predetermined levels that no one knows. On one occasion, my squad leader and I were moving quietly through customs compound to soft clear it, my radio suddenly goes off at what could be described as a yell "Bat-ter-y lev-el low, bat-ter-y lev-el twen-ty per-cent." I was also woken up one night to "Bat-ter-y lev-el cri-ti-cal, bat-ter-y level one per-cent." These three-second scream broadcasts which exceed the volume limit of the radio wouldn't be as bad if it wasn't a full, three-second broadcast of useless information. If it would simply say battery twenty percent as a normal person would, this wouldn't be as bad. The same customs compound is also where I learned a piece of invaluable information. Broken glass on a piece of sheet metal is the loudest thing you can possibly walk on. Don't ever do it. Use this information to your advantage and add it to your security.

Another Give Away

Glowing watch numbers around peoples' wrists. Not only watches but also wrist worn GPS systems. With nods, these appear to be flashing strobes as people try to sneak around in the darkness. Another huge issue with watches and phones is the alarm setting. Most attacks are carried out BMNT (Before Morning Nautical Twilight), which is a time when the rods and cones in your eyes are transitioning. Everything in the distance becomes a hazy gray which allows an enemy to walk within hand grenade range of you. BMNT is usually between 5:00 and 6:00 in the morning, the same time when many soldiers have to wake up for PT. Many of the undisciplined or forgetful would have their alarms still set. On more than one occasion, while we were on BMNT stand-to, we heard all sorts of beeps, chirps, and even music on people's alarms. This carried on at roughly 5:05, 5:25, 5:30, 5:40. Things like this can get someone killed while overseas and it led to several units being entirely rolled up in training. As you can assume, we as opposing forces, had our outer lines pre-coordinated for mortar fire and created our own personal hell for the approaching rotational unit.

A Major Asset and A Major Flaw Of Phones

Auto-brightness setting. This feature utilizes a small IR light to automatically adjust the brightness of your device. This IR strobe flashes every three seconds and under nods, will shine through clothing. When being used, the screen glow itself is bright and the strobe turns into a twenty-foot tall cone of light.

Night vision devices on rifles are also some of the devices that gave units away. They often forget to turn these forward-of-the-scope mounted devices off when moving. This paints them a nice shade of green as they move and is extremely visible under nods. While utilizing the scope, this also gives them a green ring around the eye.

There's Always The One Guy Who Thinks Life Is A Video Game

This is the dude who likes to play with his IR laser and takes pictures through his nods. This IR laser can be traced directly to the user. IR lasers are to be used only when engaging a target.

Generally a pressure switch activates the laser, a shot is fired, and the laser then turned to off. Those who don't do this give away their location. These IR lasers are frequently used to "Lasso" in helicopters at night. The large IR beam goes for miles and is used to get the attention of incoming aircraft. This way, no one has to pop a flare or give away their position to mark their location. These IR lasers, when used improperly, will quickly lead to your detriment. On one occasion, we've even seen a sniper that left his on for several minutes. Please, don't be that guy.

A Major Early Warning Is Vehicle Noise

Nothing in nature will idle like a vehicle, smell like burned gasoline, nor will it sound like the roar of rubber on a road. Tires on gravel is a noise in itself. These things, on a quiet night, can be heard for miles. If you don't believe me, travel out into a quiet spot where you can observe a highway at night. You'll know quickly what I mean. In the woods, you can hear groups of people moving and it sounds like a train. People moving in unison will create all sorts of noise from leaves crunching, sticks breaking, feet shuffling, bushes rustling, branches whining against fabric as they move by, and then the problems of trying to communicate quietly come in. A stick break does hostile make. Animals do not break sticks unless they're panicked but humans routinely do this. Evolution has taught animals to coexist with predators and remain silent. Humans dominate their environment, their weapons add confidence to them, the weight of rucksacks amplify the force of each step and carrying the light machine guns make things extremely difficult to move quietly.

Identification Friend or Foe (IFF) Markers

These range from small squares that glow under IR conditions all the way to ultra-bright IR strobes that protect them when an A/C-130 Spectre Gunship is raining hell from above. Regardless of the type, they're nods visible. Something else you won't know unless you see it is that even on black material, permanent marker is visible under nods. You'll clearly see writing even on black surfaces. We used this method on our black turtlenecks to identify ourselves from everyone else wearing solid black.

After All This, You Have The Issue Of The New Guy

No matter where you go, you have a new guy who hasn't caught on yet. By new guy, I don't mean an absolute new recruit, I mean someone that is new to operating. You could have an eighteen-year veteran of an elite unit but if this is his first time putting on kit to go slay bodies, he's going to fuck up. I've seen men that have made it into US Special Forces make absolutely stupid mistakes on their first deployment. This is where the teamwork comes in. We all guide, counsel, and support each other until we are all equally less stupid. These new guys, depending on how much time they've had before operating, just may be the guy whose phone alarm goes off inside of the target building, the guy who packed a thousand key gadgets only to forget his suppressor, or even be the dude who forgets to engage the parking brake before dismounting the vehicle. I urge you to get out there right now and be stupid. Make your mistakes, train your ass off, and go through hell. This will get your new guy stuff out of the way before it begins to matter. Train relentlessly, practice reloading every weapon in the pitch black, practice putting on your suppressor in the pitch black, know how everything functions by feel, know your equipment inside and out, practice for weapons malfunctions, practice having to change your nods batteries under pressure, and you'll quickly see how bad things can get. Hell, practice all of this after being sprayed with OC or while in a tear gas chamber. Get retarded to get smarter. Your mistakes will naturally happen until you address them and deliberately form the right habits.

Breach-Proofing

Breach-proofing is exactly as a sounds. Your enemy is going to try to get into your building by means of force, called a breach. They can use tools, a battering ram, explosives, vehicles, and whatever else they can imagine. Breach-proofing begins at the Armoring phase. Your door is only as good as the frame, the frame is only as good as the walls it's tied into, the walls are only as good as your foundation. Together, everything functions or fails as one. This comes into play more than you realize. My friend Ryan once breached a door, using me as the battering ram. He used the chest toss method and used his weight behind it. Within a second, the door stayed in place but the frame itself ripped clean out of the wall. Don't be that guy.

Never Use A Good Door And A Good Frame In Bitch-Walls

Your walls that contain necessary doors, such as the outer walls, safe room walls, or other key walls in your home should be constructed with 2"x12" studs instead of the usual 2"x4" studs. The normal spacing on most residential construction is 14 to 16 inches between studs. Your spacing should be 10 to 12 inches between studs. When those boards combined with the ballistic sandwich on the inside and regular siding on the outside, they're pretty hard to get through. Should you decide to put your ballistic sandwiches on the outside, your home will be almost impenetrable. For your 2"x12" studs, Trunks, as I call them, try to tie them in with cut pieces of boards in almost a shelving pattern between each stud. This allows great in-the-wall gear storage or a hell of a lot of insulation in a very strong wall. It won't wobble, bow, or be otherwise molested.

If you're not into this amount of lumber, try steel frame building construction. Use I-beams as studs and weld ballistic sandwiches to both the inside and the outside. Fill the inner slots with high density foam insulation or sand, and you've built a structure that will require a Cat D-10 to mess with.

Regardless, make sure your walls are prepared to accept and tie into one hell of a door frame that will be fitted, via correctional services hinges, to one hell of a door. Remember the door sandwich from the other chapter? Well, this is a good time to use it. Your door limits are your imagination. If you have the wall, frames, and hinges you can do whatever your mind can conceive. You could even take a government bunker door, put some wood on the outside of it, and use that. Your only goal is to make sure that whoever is on the other side of it, can't bust it down. Explosive charges are usually set corner to corner so that the hinges only hold a piece of the door without the knob and the other piece only has a knob to hold it.

Normally, the door will fall off on its own after a flex-linear charge. The other type of charge is a dip-can hockey puck or the wonderful donut charge. Those take out the Knob and locking mechanism by blowing a ten-inch wide whole through the entire door.

Just because you have a super wall, super frame, and super door does not mean you're done. No matter what, your door needs to swing in. Swing-out doors are destroyed easily by breaching tools and fire department tools. You'll need a way to keep it closed and the easiest way to do this are the manual sliding deadbolts. You can also pre-drill holes and leave four-inch screws in them that you can easily tighten to secure your door. If you choose to have several rotating deadbolts, make sure that there are no keyholes on the outside. Keyholes mark correct shot placement when firing .12 gauge breaching rounds. It's vital that you get good and continue to practice securing this kind of door in a hurry. Remember, you may only have a second or two to get in before the enemy is upon you, or you may have to actively struggle with an enemy to get your door closed. Which locks can you secure the fastest? Which ones are the most vital? Which ones can you secure with one hand?

Don't get stuck believing that deadbolts are only for one side of the door. Think of a vault door. You should have dead bolts that secure knob side, hinge side, the top, and the bottom, between these, you should have steel brackets installed to where you can slide a 2"x12" board at the 1/3 and 2/3 marks on the door. This makes the door as impenetrable as the wall itself. If you don't want to go through installing tree trunks into your walls, don't worry. Your regular door can still be used effectively. Just make sure that the door frame is securely tied into the wall. You can do this simply by drilling centered holes through your studs, running steel cable through, and using a cable tensioner to keep the frame secured to each and every stud. You can always install more deadbolts, add a piece of sheet steel to the back, put in brackets for even a 2"x4" board at the 1/3 and 2/3 marks, and you can still screw the door shut. If you take a 4"x4" piece of 2"x4", you can have screws pre-drilled. You place this board roughly four to six inches away from the door in its natural path of swing. This assures that every time someone kicks it, the door hits the block of wood and violently recoils back on the team, like an angry wooden spring. After the first kick, you can tell which side they're stacked up on and dump a mag through the wall and door at them.

A total mind-fuck is to take a door completely out of the equation, such as the back or side door. I recommend both. You take out the door and the frame then replace the open space with studs. You then re-do your inner drywall. On the outside, you will have your door. You knock the inner side of the knob off entirely and make sure it sits flush to the wall. You screw it in place using four-inch screws to the studs of the wall behind it. You then set-up decorative framework around it. Now, you have a solid door, screwed to a solid wall, that looks as if it might swing open. Once a breach team shows up, they'll be pounding the hell out of the back wall which, to you, it's like a polite way of letting you know you have company. Should they flex-linear charge it, the door will remain on the wall and the wall will still stand.

If you want to play with a breach team, you do something similar. You put a paper thin door up with no drywall behind it, the whole fake door frame routine, and wait. Once a breach team shows up, they'll end up kicking through the door completely and often be stuck with their foot coming through an open space in your wall. While good for comedic relief, they can still come through this hole.

Next, Windows

Look at your residential building code and you'll realize that the window is almost free-floating to allow the home to shift with the seasons. This is the next preferred breach point. A battering ram will often knock a window frame out of the wall with a well-placed strike to the bottom. You remedy this while still allowing window shift by opening the walls around the window. You drill holes in the middle of each stud, generally three or four studs on each side of the window. You also do this to the top and bottom of the window. You slide cables through the holes, and you use tensioners to keep the wall and window frame tied together. These thin cables will not break and should a breach team knock one out, it will quickly spring back into place. If you have windows, you should have pre-cut pieces of one-inch plywood with pre-drilled holes that match perfectly to the inner window frame. At the first sign of trouble, you button up your home by placing these window covers up with four-inch screws, lock all your doors, and prepare for war.

You can add to your security by using magnetic alarms on the windows and doors, but beware, these alarms can malfunction and they're also incredibly easy to bypass. They also make a horrible sound, regardless of why the window or door is being opened. For this reason, I don't like them unless I'm installing them during the lockdown phase of the plan. Then, anything that slides or swings the door open is absolutely coming in to take me out. At that point, there's no denying it and it provides a great early warning.

There are a variety of other small security systems that can be researched thoroughly online that will tie in with full home security systems. Just remember, anyone coming in to install such an item will then know exactly what you have in your home, may want to steal it, and may even be dumb enough to try to come back. I've had several cable guys and maintenance crews comment on the amount of firearms I had readily available in the apartment. I've never trusted these folks and I don't believe that I ever will.

Yard Hell

Now that you know your home is going to take forever to get into, you can start planning for your yard. Specifically, what will prevent them from getting to the house, what will they do after they fail a breach. What will they do if they take fire on approach, and what will they do in response to bullets flying through walls or gunports? By knowing this, you can have extra measures prepared to keep them at bay, slow down reinforcements, and take them out while they're in retreat. Sympathize with your enemy. They've had to go through hellish thorns, all sorts of early warning devices and traps, and now they're ready to begin the assault. They're likely sore, angry, and frustrated which you can use to your advantage. Several things can slow them down on approach. Shotguns with rock-salt loads, nails in the yard, punji pits, trip wires, an electrified chicken wire layer that covers your yard, sprinkler systems filled with diesel fuel on a pressure tank that can be lit with a flare gun, propane jets with igniters facing your door, all sorts of things can quickly make them think twice about coming in and continue to give them hell on their retreat. You can turn your hand railings on the stairs into a propane jet by drilling holes, use carpet to conceal false stairs, use dead-falls, and all sorts of traps.

The slips, trips, falls, electrocutions, severe burns, rock-salt injuries, operators stuck in bear traps, flashing lights and IR torches, and whatever other hell you can think of bringing them will be a massive hit to their ego. You simply put them into hell and you're the devil. In the pain, frustration, and confusion, you can fire at them with almost complete impunity. If they retreat, remember that they're a valid enemy that are trying to rob or kill you. Bullet range should be their only safety.

Remember, when they're on approach, you are in control, and you get to choose when to strike. You choose when to activate your strobes, electrify the toys, activate the sprinklers, and when to kick off the show. There's also no rules saying that all of this has to be in your immediate vicinity. You can have a diesel pump set up out in the woods and activate it based on your camera feed, set up traps further out, dig a moat, dig a giant snake pit, have all sorts of fences put up, your limit is once again your imagination. The farther they have to go to get you, the less dedicated will quickly fall back or retreat as soon as things get real. You need to demoralize them before you ever have to fight them. You want them hurt, exhausted, and thinking they'll never see their family again by the time they get anywhere near you.

With everything properly in place, you should never have to fire a shot. You should make them question whether or not you're even in the building. You never reveal anything unless you have to.

Let's assume that these men absolutely want to take you prisoner. They'll stop at nothing to get you. These are the ones that will make it through the waves of hell, pull back their casualties, and begin thinking of how to exploit your weakness. They've persevered through the hell, the failed breach, watching their buddies get shredded, caught in bear traps, electrocuted, and shot through walls only to be pushed back.

Their only plan at that point is to regroup, reinforce, and make sure they can't fail. You're up against a tactical badass who is planning a front door, back door, and two simultaneous window breaches. All of which are explosive, except the main door which is going to be brought down by an armored vehicle. They've dotted every I, crossed every T, have medical support and extraction vehicles on standby, the ICU at their field hospital is prepped, and they're dedicated to going in. The best of the best thinkers have every single detail mapped out.

The teams are all in place, everything is flawless, then it begins. The team in back blew the fake door in half only to find your solid wall, the window teams found out the hard way that the frame and one-inch plywood are going nowhere, but the armored vehicle, traveling at 25 mph, has busted through your front wall. Their back ramp has dropped and now you have enemies piling out to kill you. So, what do you do? This next section is dedicated to what you should have in place around the house, long before it's ever needed.

Hell In The House

Once again, because of your superior education, research skills, and preparation, you've fortified your home to ensure that anyone who manages to get in, won't be coming out. You've extended your fatal funnel and placed obstacles in it to botch their breach, strong walled every interior wall that faces the main breach point, added specific gunports, and you're now firing from a covered position. You can safely mag dump without fear of being hit in the process. But, how did you get to this safe, confident position? By doing the following:

Every wall that faces your weak point (in this case, the main door to the home which is also the only room with windows in it) you've added a ballistic sandwich with several gun ports so that you can engage from cover. You've assured that your walls are properly cable tied in, and you set up absolute mind games.

Your home is your castle, and you should dominate it always. This is your turf, your job is to defend your life, your family, and your property against invading threats.

Breaching houses is one hell of a fun task, but much can go wrong. Split second decisions make all the difference once you're through the door and in the fatal funnel. Every barrel in the room is on you and your only hope is to have lightning-fast movements, absolute dexterity, have a perfectly functioning weapon, be able to see, hear, smell, and taste everything within a second. Being able to see where the enemy is at, identify potential traps, identify obstacles, and call "short room" is vital for situational awareness. Everything gets verbally called out, "door right, window left, window right, dead-space behind the couch" or the normal things. Shoot holes, IEDs, and other surprises are entirely unexpected. Identifying and vocalizing them are a hell of a task. These small details are what can give the operators a sensory overload and the main reason why we train in every environment. Whether it be plywood villages, villages constructed of shipping containers, actual buildings, our barracks, shoot houses at ranges, survival ranches, or in each of our friends' houses, the changing environment helps us function together. You will learn body language of your team fast and even the minute gestures will speak paragraphs. Once everyone has everything fluid from each position of the stack, the process quickly advances. Multiple rooms, multiple buildings, multiple floors, different breach points. We personally stay frosty in mechanical breaches using a variety of tools, shotgun breaches, vehicle breaches where a long battering ram projects from the frame, explosive breaches using a few different charges, body breaches which are pretty self-explanatory, failed or multi-method breaching, and a scary-as-hell situation when the door opens as you stack up on it.

Everything comes into play. The number of locks, the construction of the door, likely presence of enemies, likeliness of traps on the door, and visibility of the door all come into play. If there's no previous surveillance of the buildings and doors, these decisions are made on the fly by an already over-worked team leader. Many mistakes can happen throughout this complex process and it's your job to monopolize on this.

Take Their Sight

The first mind game is to assure that they can't see. If it's a night raid, this is where flashing strobes come in handy to assure that it's both too bright to see through nods and too dark to see with the naked eyes. This is where all sorts of party lights come into play, preferably ultra-bright LEDs and IR strobes that alternate flashes.

If it's a day raid, having a smoke screen is a huge asset, especially in a small enclosure such as a living room. Another asset is to pressurize OC or CS gas and have the exhaust fill the target room. There's nothing like stepping out of an armored vehicle only to become doused in liquid hell. You take their ability to breathe in your home, they'll quickly leave it. You can also rig up pepper-ball launchers to pneumatic switches to begin firing bursts with the flick of a switch. This adds physical pain to the already hellish heat of your deterrent. Failing OC and CS, a simple pressure washer filled with ghost pepper oil will suffice. There are several other things that border on the verge of chemical weapons that you can use as well but we won't be discussing that sort of sort of thing here.

Take Their Communications, The Fun Way

Have a stereo system installed throughout the house. Play your favorite music, or a sadistic tune, to set the mood and stop them from using their radios or even yelling to each other. The pain threshold for sound sets in at 130 decibels and competition stereos can quickly exceed 200. With this level of system installed into the small enclosures of your rooms, this can quickly become disorienting, make an enemy physically sick, and cause an inability to function depending on what frequencies you're blasting. This asset also helps you mask your own movement and if you're shooting suppressed, the enemy may not even know they're under fire until half their team is dead. At that level of volume, they may not even hear unsuppressed shots. There are several available frequency jammers available but beware, these devices are banned by the FCC and are a federal offense to use. However, once society collapses and it means the difference between life and death, the law won't really matter.

The government will be in such a state of chaos from the chaotic enemy presence that they, too, will be resorting to outside-the-law options. As they say, a fair fight is a lost fight. Don't be the dead man who fought fair.

Play With Their Breachers

Cardboard cutouts of armed individuals are life-sized and are frequently used at shooting ranges. You can also put up mannequins and wire-framed uniforms that are pointing weapons at the fatal funnel. Realistic enough targets on the wall may also work. The goal is to get the breachers to slow down in the fatal funnel and engage the silhouettes while you engage from a covered and concealed position, preferably on the other side of a ballistic sandwiched wall.

For hallways, the easiest option is to staple high test fishing line into the studs on each side. While a team is moving through your home, they'll likely be in a strong-wall formation or a T formation. Once you hear them get caught up in the fishing line, they're essentially stuck so you can engage them at your leisure.

A roll-out carpet with nails in it is a great way to slow down traffic until the obstacle is cleared, another option is nail punji under a carpet. You have a few floorboards pre-removed and have a bed of nails facing up under it. The boards stay in place when not needed and to activate your trap, simply remove the boards and wait for the carpet to be stepped on. Just be sure that the carpet will smoothly conform to the space, or it won't bend, therefore not allowing the enemy's foot to reach the hell. Remember the recoiling door? This is an effective tool to use in each room you enter. You can also tie doors shut with rope, staple them shut, screw them shut, oil the floors, anything to make each and every breach a nightmare for the team. A little known fact is that if they have to struggle, they may consider simply destroying the home. However, if they're there to detain you, they'll refrain from risking your life. Many robbers also do not want to catch a murder charge so that can also be used to your advantage.

The Maze

Your house should be built or restricted in movement so that it forms a continuous loop from the front doors all the way to your egress point. Make sure that each room only has one entrance and one exit. If there's a room with doors leading to two rooms, permanently seal one of them and keep the maze going. The last thing you want is for multiple points of exit for your enemy. They're in your house, it's your job to make sure that they never leave. By building a circuit pattern, you assure that the enemy isn't coming from behind and that you continually lead them deeper into your house. Once your back is against the wall, only you know this, and it can be a huge advantage. The only "dead ends" should be closets with actual room doors on them to fool enemies. Try to keep your rooms flowing from one to the other, get rid of hallway-fed room doors. Put the doors where they can only be accessed by you, provided that you've already passed the point of entry. You want your enemy to be trapped in hallways because they're narrow, a room would allow them to flee from your hail of gunfire.

Whatever may be coming at you, whether it be an angry mob, wild groups of looters, rogue tactical tams, raging drug dealers, rioters, or an invading military force, the procedure is the same. You need to inflict as many casualties as fast as you can to get them out of your home. Having multiple reinforced doors throughout your home is key to slowing them down, restricting their movement, and allowing you to refocus your energy back to casualty producing. While on the run, you're not an effective war fighter.

The End Game

How do you plan to finish the engagement? If you're severely out-numbered and you know they're going to come in, this is where having a safe room in the basement would come in handy. The situation would be a basement only accessible from the closet floor that you can get in and out of. You should also have a tunnel that runs a few hundred feet out to safety so that you can egress. The point of this is to fake your own death or at least delay their ability to prove your survival for several hours. You do this effectively by keeping ten gallon buckets of diesel fuel in each room. As you see that room begins to fall and you're forced to leave, you open the top and shove it over as you exit. You get the team to chase you all the way to the end of your maze, continuing to tip over your pre-positioned diesel buckets. Once you reach your escape hatch into your basement/bunker, you tip your last barrel, fire a flare into the room and button down your hatch. You set final traps in your enclosure and run out the tunnel. The house is now burning with them inside it and the fire will continue to spread, sealing them from discovering where you've disappeared to. If you can fool them into believing that you're dead, even for a while, you can get away.

It's important to plan for your egress and rehearse it regularly so that it's a second nature. Get familiar with your traps, your methods of slowing them down, how you plan to move, and where you plan to shoot from. I'm not going to go far into detail on booby-traps due to the sensitive nature of the subject and wide variety of published sources on the subject. The more you can safely employ, the better off you'll be when the time comes to actually use these skills.

What you've so far read is the absolute worst case scenario. A scenario that any gang, band of hoodlums, robbers, thieves, burglars, or any other undesirables will avoid doing. As I said in the beginning, this book is about facing the worst of the worst in a tactical scenario. Nearly a force on force situation. Not only you, but your family may also be engaging the enemy alongside you. It is absolutely vital that each of you can communicate with the insane noise, rehearsing the plan until you're sick of it will really pay off once you realize that you can't hear, are under fire, and that you may have a casualty.

Once you think you're good, discuss the weak points of your plan and try to put counter-measures in place to mitigate the danger. Something as simple as a table in a certain place, a quickly placed trap, an additional door-reinforcement, and other on-the-fly toys can be a real life saver.

It is important to know that no one is omnipotent. You can be the best special operations operative in the world with fifteen deployments, hundreds of personal kills, and absolutely super-human skill but when the first round fired by the enemy strikes your skull, it's game over. Your job is to detect the enemy and dodge that bullet before it's even fired. If not, you've gone through a hellish life of intense experiences for absolutely nothing at all.

Now that you know several tools to make it out alive, we're going to go into the necessary steps to get out of the area undetected.

Chapter 4

Evasion

Now that you've managed to get away from the situation or whether you simply realized that an enemy is actively seeking you, it's now time to evade them as if your life depended on it, because it does.

There is no simple answer for what you will have to do next, but you will have to continuously react to your ever changing environment. The smallest things can alert an enemy to your presence, whether it be a scorned neighbor, a shopkeeper that you've had foul words with, spies, snitches, or fatal mistakes of being seen. After this happens, whether or not you know about it, you have a very short time to get away.

Should your enemy have a dominating presence in the area that has cultivated sympathizers, they'll try to create an "Us versus Them" mentality. Their followers, stool pigeons and sheep really, will associate themselves close to the enemy and form an "Us" relationship. They'll accept the enemy as the new form of government as long as suffering is sufferable. This leaves them to paint you and your followers as "Them" which are the outsiders, the radicals, the lunatics, and extremists in their eyes. Stupid people are easily duped into following and it's not entirely their fault. Public education can enhance these views of socialism, communism, and even fascism through propaganda, politically correct doctrines, and outright lies. The other side can enhance views of capitalism, conservatism, closed mindedness, and general hatred. If you're in the middle, you're rejected by both as a dissenter.

Keep up with the local news channels and they'll often reveal to you who the rebels are, who the collaborators are, and who remains neutral with hidden motives. Knowing where riots, protests, public executions of certain groups, marching radicals, and foreign tensions can be an early warning on what to do, where to go, and who to pretend to be in certain areas.

From our point of view, we are the "Us" and the enemy is the "Them." Anyone who is not "Us" is a snitch, plain and simple. Even the slightest sympathizing comments betray the mind of the opinion holder. Years in federal prison have taught me that anyone, anywhere, can turn you in for anything. Even fictitious evidence that the "Them" can't ignore. If they have a reason, they'll turn on you.

In the world, people want your job, the respect level you've earned, your vehicle, the way you live, your spouse, and anything else that is better than what they have. They will stop at nothing to snake you, hit you from angles where they think they can remain anonymous, snitch on you to the enemy, or may start vicious rumors in hopes that your family will abandon you. Some may sell you out just to raid your property before the enemy has a chance to go through it all. Some may even want to prove their loyalty to the enemy simply for extra privileges or earn a higher position of trust amongst them. You have not seen the level of scum-baggery that will ensue.

You must play the role that you've selected at all times. Whether it's hipster, college kid, honest businessman, innocent farmer, your role is your life in front of the enemy. One small slip and your entire world may come crashing down. Imagine seeing someone you thought of for years as a humble gas station cashier. In a moment of strife, they began firing rapid pairs into a group of attackers, maintain a perfect c-clamp, and reload like a badass. You'll quickly realize that the man was not simply a gas station attendant. Imagine seeing a woman approached in an alley who looks innocent or feeble, only to body slam an assailant twice her size and finish him off with a Diver's stiletto. Those perfectly executed tasks take practice, familiarity, and confidence that only dedicated training can provide.

Your situational awareness is key to staying under the radar. You have to know who is around, calculate the threat level someone poses, and whether to feign the innocent victim or cripple an assailant. The two people mentioned above will be thoroughly investigated. Those skills stand out to anyone who knows what to look for. Sometimes, it's better to give up a decoy wallet and let people think you got robbed. There are times when there are others around and you should play the victim as long as it doesn't pose a serious threat to you or your family. Should you have to react in front of people, don't immediately kick off and reveal your training. Box with a boxer, roll with a roller, and try to repel them by other means. The training you receive is for when absolutely necessary to protect lives.

This comes in handy for a number of reasons. The most important is that the police only need probable cause to enter your home. If they know what you have or possess even an inkling of hatred towards them, you may find yourself in a very bad position. Should their authority be lawful, they maybe confiscate things from you or paint you as a public threat. When law enforcement raided my apartment, using a map drawn by my roommate, they were quick to gather my legally owned firearms, my legally owned plate carriers, my legally owned helmets, the gear I was lawfully issued and required by the United States Army to maintain in good condition, my notebooks from counter-IED courses from overseas, and other items to paint me as an armed madman. At the time, I was a government loyalist who obeyed the laws, yet they still painted me in that light. Notes that helped protect our lives overseas were skewed into "bomb plans" in the eyes of the government. My legally owned firearms and tactical gear were used to paint a picture of me being the next active shooter. My issued gear that I was required to maintain was used to paint the same picture, a Vernon Parish detective even went as far as to assert that "soldiers are not supposed to keep this in their home" which is a crock of shit and contrary to regulation. Service members are issued thousands of dollars of gear and they maintain it in their home. The government, in no way, is ever required to furnish us lockers for our issued equipment. They maintain our issued firearms, communication equipment, and the property of the United States Army. Not our personal equipment. Let this be a clean and clear lesson, the government is about money, not loyalty.

Let that sink in. I was a government loyalist with two combat deployments to Afghanistan, was up for promotion to Sergeant, and was about to go on my third deployment, all within five years of service. They painted me as an armed lunatic based on what I lawfully owned and was issued by the United States Government. Now, it is true that a few thousand dollars of the equipment was "off the books" meaning that it had been stolen after being shifted in responsibility or turned in. Accountability of those items were no longer required so we simply took things home. Let this be a lesson. If the government can see it, they're going to get nervous. If you're doing anything wrong at all, you're a threat in their eyes.

Relocate to an area with fewer cops. In times of chaos or conflict, the cops might come under fire. This deadly, all-direction hail of gunfire can quickly become dangerous to everyone around. Try to be nowhere near it. Cops can also be a pain in the ass when they are following orders that they don't understand. Look into all the civil rights cases surrounding the police. Now, imagine that you're on the receiving end of this without a legal remedy, in a time of chaos.

Once you're confident about the area you're in, it pays to know what is going on and the best way to do this is enemy comms. Get ahold of their radios any way you can and stash it somewhere for a while. Some radios have GPS function, and the enemy will quickly try to regain their equipment. There is also a huge factor that will get you caught up. The big orange button. On military radios, the big orange button is the "zero" button which turns the radio into a useless brick. It erases everything on the radio. On police radios, the orange button is the body alarm. This activates a distress signal with their headquarters and assures that every officer in the area knows that one is in immediate danger. Essentially, everyone that can hear the call will be swarming on you from every direction. "When one blue goes down, everyone blue goes to help."

Should your enemy operate on similar plans, you'll either be left with a brick or covered in enemies. So, be careful. Get the model number and try to look at the manuals for the radios, just be careful when ordering them.

You can still use the body alarm to your advantage. You can set the radio in a rival's area and press the body alarm. Every enemy in the area is going to enter the premises and discover what is in it. Should you ever get a hold of a cop's radio and happen to know where the local pedophile ring is at, this is a sure way to get cops in there with no warrant needed. Have fun and remember to use things wisely.

Staging

Learn how your enemy stages before operations. Should there be a large force planning an assault, they'll meet up someplace to go over the plans, make sure each element is ready, do final weapons checks and then begin the operation. If you know that your enemy prefers to meet in public parking lots within a block of the target, you can use this to your advantage and put drop cameras and cover the parking lots around you. If you know that they don't stage at all, but they only roll out in a convoy for a raid operation, you watch that door with a drop camera and begin your evacuation plan, staying out of the area until you're sure that you're not the intended target.

Know When You're In Danger

Red flags fly before things get bad. You know in the movies when you see the cartel getting their guns ready, pictures of the target get passed around, and you see them all gathering to assault? Well, those are the same red flags you see in life, but they are far less dramatic. By noticing what it looks like when the enemy is conducting operations, you can determine when to run, when to fight, and when to not move a muscle.

Red flags are normally excessive radio chatter or the complete absence of chatter. If they're requiring a lot of chatter, they won't be on the main frequency. Their main one will be dead while another channel is usually giving a play-by-play. You'll hear their radio checks, operations start word, the checkpoints they're using along the route, the call signs of each element, and other necessary chatter. Since there's no clear indicator of what the target will be everything is in danger until proven not. Local evacuations are a sign that someone in authority is going to conduct a raid and doesn't want anyone but their target to be harmed.

When you see outer cordons, roadblocks, drones, or helicopter passes, you know that something big is going on, something where they expect a runner. When you see people start leaving the area, bringing their children in from play, and an eerie feeling, you know what time it is. If cell service shuts down in your area, this may be a strategic play in order to make sure that no one in the area can communicate enemy presence. It is also commonplace to shut down the power of a target building or even buildings in the vicinity to ensure that the target is blind. If your power goes out and no one else's does, this may be a sign. If everyone's goes out, you should still be ready for anything. Cutting the power is also to ensure your cameras are out. At H-hour, where the enemy actually begins their operation, you'll see the immediate signs. Vehicles speeding into the area, tires screeching to a halt, lots of rapid footsteps, flash-bang grenades, and gunfire are commonplace in a fast-paced raid. The assault element normally tries to move faster than anyone trying to alert the target and they doing this by far exceeding the speed limit. You may see a convoy of vehicles doing 40 mph in a 25 mph zone, come screeching to a halt only feet from the front door of the target building, and barrel through the door like a horde of hungry dogs. Things get aggressive. The 1.5 second fuse on a flash-bang feels as if it takes an hour before going off. They're pissed that the flash-bang hasn't incapacitated everyone inside, and they get extremely rough with everyone in the building, regardless of who they are.

Even in training, we have an aggression for people in rooms. I've personally been picked up, slammed, tossed around, and dragged, and gagged by room clearers. Now, imagine this aggression from an enemy that's coming into a hostile environment. Things get noisy, sloppy, and violent at the first second. Seeing this will reveal to you their professionalism, tactics, and the reason why you don't want them anywhere near your place for any reason.

If you're on the run, where would you find you? Where would your family find you? Where would your friends find you? By answering these questions, you now know where your enemy will find you. By knowing your family and friends, that enemy can exploit their care for you, their need to contact you, and their need to see you. Inadvertently, your family and friends may be your downfall so you should consider having places that only you know about. Should it be a barbaric enemy, they'll all be tortured for information. They simply cannot give up what they don't know. As you will see in a later chapter, the enemy will work off of a torture schedule so your family will endure it whether they talk or not.

Next question is where would the government find you? The enemy will use these same places as traps. Banks, safe deposit boxes, jobs, known properties, and associates are all exploitable when looking for someone. The easiest way to track anyone is through their financial energy and tax records. You wouldn't believe the places that your Social Security number is associated with right now. Plenty of companies, their contracted employees, information brokers, and anyone who wants to defraud you will have this information easily available to them.

Resupply

Should society collapse, you'll have to take a good look into everything that you need and want. Eventually these supplies will run out, so it pays to stock up early. Where can you get all of the supplies that you need to survive happily? Where can you go without being seen? Believe it or not, you may end up doing midnight raids on sporting goods stores, surplus stores, gun shops, grocery stores, and distributors. If society has completely degraded into lawlessness, you may consider raiding the former Police Department, National Guard Armory, police safe-houses that are no longer in use, warehouses, and other high value targets that are sure to have a big yield. Have you ever been in a beverage distributor or food service warehouse? You'll quickly see the advantages to saying hello to one with the moving truck. You should live happily for years if you "shop" right. Personally, I like to know where the drug dealers are at and those are my primary target should I decide to begin a Viking campaign against neighborhoods. I don't believe in robbing innocent people, so I choose to keep track of the social scum that plagues our neighborhoods. The drug dealers, the troublesome, the wanna-be gangsters. At least the very least, their dead bodies will yield weapons, plenty of weapons.

Let's go out on the "what if" for a minute. Let's say that you are exposed entirely. Enemy intelligence paid a carton of cigarettes to a snitch and now they know everything. They know your home, your bug out locations, and where your supplies are stored. They're sure to have a sniper at or at least a surveillance team posted to each of these locations since they see you as a direct threat to their operations. The snitches painted you as a man of insanity, the vigilante citizen of mayhem and their operations are your main anarchist target at which to channel your explosives stockpile. Worse yet, their vehicles are quickly rolling up on you.

What should you have done to prepare for this? The first step is vehicle modifications. If you can't get home or to your locations, your vehicle is all you have. Are you prepared to live in this environment? Can you thrive happily within the confines of your vehicle? Let's take some steps into what you can do to a vehicle to add simple luxuries.

Your first goal is to not stand out. All of your modifications should have nothing to do with the appearance of the vehicle. The last thing you want is to have a small battle-wagon that everyone wants to kill you for. You want a good vehicle that's fuel efficient. My little Ford Ranger was a five-speed manual from 2002. I turned it into a beast, and I recommend that you do something similar.

Get an older vehicle so that you know what the general problems are and be prepared to fix them over and over. Get yourself plenty of spare parts and know the vehicle inside and out. Put in aftermarket parts that make your vehicle more efficient, run smoother, and allow whatever sort of performance modifications that you want. Look into things like a seriously powerful engine, high performance chips which allow you to customize every aspect of your vehicle, superchargers and turbo chargers (learn which you prefer), high performance alternators, high performance transmissions, how you want your rear differential geared, suspension, shocks or coil-overs, and almost every aspect of functions under the hood. Extremely reliable parts can be found for everything under your hood, in the body of your vehicle, and underneath. Some of them can be lifesavers, just make sure you know its impact on the vehicle.

As for toys, you can get a wide variety of light bars of every color LED imaginable, some of which allow you to see as if you were driving in the day. Some are full light bars which span your whole roof whereas others are made to be installed into the grille of your vehicle. The short ones can be converted to directional lights and put almost anywhere.

Your whole center console can be replaced with a variety of aftermarket consoles, some of which have built in power ports, holsters, hiding compartments, several compartments, layered compartments, or anything you can think of. These can be custom designed for you as well.

Some modifications and even aftermarket seats allow you to have a 100 gallon fuel tank discreetly hidden, several firearms, or anything else you can think of. The possibilities are limitless, and you can always resort to custom builds, removing whole seats, or even adding a bed.

A good idea that will help almost any situation is the ability to use ruggedized tires that make it hard to get stuck while off roading, a two to four-inch lift kit, a snorkel kit, and a custom-cut ballistic sandwich to cover your back as needed. These ballistic sandwiches can be used to fit neatly into the trunk to protect your whole back seat, cut to replace the back wall of a truck, or something cut to the shape of your seats to guard you from direct shots. Weight could be an issue with these so you may only need a piece of 1/8 inch steel on a half-inch sheet of plywood.

You can get a variety of run-flat technology for all styles of tires and even Kevlar-walled tires. These things can come in handy not only for gunfighting but for off-roading in general. You can also remove your door panels and line your doors with Kevlar. When you replace the door panel, you can't tell the door has been modified except for the extra weight.

You can also look into vehicle armoring companies that turn your family's sedan into a battlewagon. They can go from level one which is simply reinforcing parts, to level seven, which is basically a bulletproof capsule slid into your frame, all the way to level 12 which is the Beast Presidential Limousine. After you've got your things in order, be sure to try everything out, know your new fuel efficiency rating, and then you have some fun.

Fun begins with the offense. Things like oil-slick, caltrops, flame-throwers, OC sprayers, built-in under-the-hood shotguns, and many other toys are not just for the movie industry. You can use these things in a pursuit to lose your enemy or completely disable them.

Multiple Vehicles

You should have one vehicle that's an armed-to-the-teeth battlewagon that's kept in a hidden garage. One for the rough times when your security needs to be elevated, and one pursuit car.

Your battle-wagon is the vehicle with reinforced everything, high performance parts, your full bug out arsenal, and weapons mounted throughout. This vehicle is the one with the ultra-bright LED light bars, red and blue emergency flashers, pursuit weapons, double fuel tank, and maybe even a pintle for a heavy machine gun mounted to it.

You use the rough times vehicle for everyday use which contains your medic bag, roadside emergency kit, bug out bag, full tool set, and your firearms. This is your everyday, subtle vehicle to get you around safely.

Your pursuit car is an older compact vehicle with a lot of under the hood work, no passenger seat, no back seats, and an empty trunk. The pursuit car is for you to get into a place, do what you need to do, and get out. It's intentionally kept empty and absolutely slick to achieve maximum speed. The trunk is kept empty so that you can suddenly stop, pop the trunk, and release a hail of unobstructed gunfire into a pursuer.

With the battle-wagon, think of a vehicle that you'd be willing to fight in. I prefer a larger truck such as a Ram with a replaced back wall, Kevlar in the doors, machine gun pintle on the roof, full roll cage, light bars on the roof and push bar, and all sorts of performance modifications. The side panels and bodywork are replaced with diamond plate aluminum, scuffed and camouflaged of course. Generally a four-inch lift and 35 inch all-terrain tires. The tailgate is a ballistic sandwich, and all of your survival supplies are ratchet strapped down in the bed. Your absolutely necessary supplies ride in the back on top of the 100 gallon diesel tank. The make and model of your vehicle should suit you well, something that you can work on easily and that you're familiar with. I've seen everything from armored mini Coopers, full-sized Humvees, Ford F-450s, buses, station wagons, and Dodge Chargers. As long as it's suitable for local terrain, terrain of your bug out location, and efficient enough in fuel to get there, you're good to go. Get creative and have yourself some fun in the garage.

The daily driver is something that you want to keep stocked with your supplies and your full emergency kit. This is the vehicle that you'll be driving to and from work. This is the vehicle you will handle unexpected emergencies in and the vehicle that you'll be seen in most often. Your friends and enemies will both know it, so it pays to keep it looking like a normal car. My daily drivers were my 2002 Ford Ranger and my 2008 Toyota Corolla. For the truck, I kept all of my tools and supplies in the barely existent backseat and right there with my stereo setup. It was a toolkit, tow straps, aid bag, bug out bag, my Breacher's 870, and extra Glock 19 with 10 mags, roadside emergency kit, ax and hatchet, folding shovel, pry bar, folding saw, a 10-inch Kicker subwoofer, my amplifier, blankets, and extra snacks. In the bed, I kept a few gallons of coolant, a few quarts of oil, in the spare tire, and a tough box full of extra supplies.

Beware of pursuit immobilizing techniques such as driving tactics, electronic interference devices, and what the enemiy's vehicles are capable of. Their PIT may consist of sweeping the rear of the car to the side, boxing you in on each side then applying their brakes, forming a full box around you, taking out your tires, hooking onto your vehicle, and several other tricks depending on who you are up against. Electronic interference devices can range from having your vehicle's computer disabled remotely, EMP projectiles, simple and GPS tags, and other cool toys from Disable-U-Shack. It also pays to know who you can outrun, which of your enemies know how to drive, and who is dedicated enough to follow you through a hail of gunfire. If you can't outrun them, shoot them.

When Running Isn't Effective

Whether you're on foot or in a vehicle, it's important to know how to evade the enemy, how to disable them, how to out-maneuver them, how to outsmart them, and how to not get involved in a pursuit in the first place.

While on foot, there are several things you can do to do get away from a pursuing enemy. We'll start with the nicer things to do. Your first idea is the most obvious, disappear into a crowd of people. Your enemy will rarely ever shoot into a crowd to stop you so you can use them for cover. It is important that you gauge their professionalism and their reactions though. Your enemy may, in fact, utilize tactics of "shoot them and anyone they use for cover." An enemy like this does not care who gets killed so you should avoid running into crowds against these people. Unless the crowd are enemy supporters. Then, they'll see that the enemy doesn't care about them either and may switch to the right side. Remember back in the day when the Irish Republican Army set off bombs all over Belfast, killing many innocents, children, and harming local businesses? They were quickly met with angry responses and switched their tactics.

A bit more aggressive of an approach is to quickly round a corner and assail your pursuer with a blunt object. These are things you could have on you, things you had staged in a dead drop or an object you've picked up in the pursuit. Once they round the corner, you use their momentum to make your first strike more effective. Aim for the lower jaw, throat, knees, and ankles. A solid hit to either of these will stop your pursuer. Should your pursuer be dedicated or scared, they'll likely escalate to lethal force. Wait until they present their firearm and monopolize on this opportunity to gain control of it. If there's more than one pursuer, it may benefit you to inflict as much damage as possible to each but never let them get close to you. Your objective on foot is to get away from them as fast as possible.

You can always double back, which is where you abruptly stop and let them pass you. This allows you to get into a position of dominance over them since you are now behind them, but it also gives you the opportunity to slip through their immediate cordon.

The most aggressive option is to round a corner, stop abruptly and have your pistol meet their face as they round the corner. Smoke them and anyone behind them. You can also knee-cap them with a round then run in a safe direction. They'll quickly tell their friends which direction you ran, and this is precisely while you'll change directions after losing their sight. This pretty well ends the pursuit there until they can reorganize and reinforce. You can also time how far back they are and drop a grenade, take them on a route that you already have traps set-up in, or take them through a door that locks from the outside. Once they're trapped in a building, they're under your complete control and mercy.

There are opportunities almost anywhere for you to turn into a business, hide in someone's yard, pass through all sorts of obstacles, and disappear. Just beware that with someone on foot, they will set-up a perimeter and quickly start to box you in. You must far exceed their ability to continue if you want to escape or have a plan to become a floorboard as they search the hiding place that you're trying to use. Just avoid being pushed into an ambush or into a roadblock they set up.

Actions While Mobile

If you're tired of running, it's time to get mobile. Since you're a competent prepper, let's assume that you have your regular vehicle and your pursuit car close by. Your regular vehicle is probably compromised and currently your enemy has a sniper waiting on you to return to it. Since everyone knows your regular vehicle, it's time to use the pursuit car to get out of there in a hurry.

If you do not have a clear path to get out of the area, you better know how to drive. Once the enemy locks on their cordon, you're not getting out of it in a vehicle so it's vital to get out as soon as possible. Get as far away as you can, as fast as you can.

Should the enemy stop you in your pursuit car before they actually know who you are, it's a good time to fake surrender. Your face should reflect genuine concern and your hands should be up in an innocent manner. If they already have guns drawn on you, this is an easy way to make anyone who is not in the loop comfortable around you. You never pull a gun on guns that are already drawn on you. Wait for your opportunity and monopolize on it. Depending on what you're carrying, they might not find your pistol if they search you. You need to be the snake in the grass until you can get rid of them and get moving.

If they're in pursuit of your vehicle, you can outdrive them, outrun them, or outsmart them. If neither of these will work and you know it, stop abruptly and throw your parking brake on. You hop out and begin spraying rounds through their windshield. Generally, you'll have to dump the whole mag into the same area to achieve round penetration due to the many layers of laminated glass. If they have ballistic glass, spider it with rounds so that the driver cannot see.

If they're on to this tactic, switch to shooting through the open trunk. This allows you to effectively engage a target without having to worry about spent brass tying you to the scene.

What You Should Begin Today

There are several things you can do to make yourself an effective artist of evasion. When it comes to shooting from a vehicle, people are generally not well practiced at this. Don't be discouraged though, we're going to tear up some land.

The first thing you need to think of is mounted react to contact. Put targets all around your vehicle at varying ranges and roll down all of your windows. Practice engaging these targets from within your vehicle using a wide variety of firearms. You should be able to use a rifle, pistol, and shotgun from every position of the vehicle effectively. This involves shooting through all four window spaces of your vehicle. Don't worry about the rear window or the windshield. These windows generally take a whole magazine to punch through and you obviously cannot roll them down for practice. However, you can take an old beater vehicle out to the woods and practice this in depth.

Once you get good at shooting from each position, practice your driving skills and combine them. Set up targets on a range and do several drills. In one, you stop right before your targets and dismount to engage them. In another drill, your vehicle is pre-parked in front of the targets, and you practice hopping out of each door to engage targets. When in the back, rehearse dismounting alone and then practice your shots while the driver or passenger door is open. This gets you familiar with having the obstructions there so when there's a person behind this door, you know how to shoot around them safely. Then, you do the same drills with the targets to the sides and rear of the vehicle so that you get used to dismounting contact side, firing over the vehicle, and firing without the door to use for support or cover.

Once you feel confident in this, have your people do the same. Once everyone is familiar with how to safely handle a weapon inside the vehicle, fire from windows, and dismount to engage targets, you begin adding people to the car. The final interaction involves a person in each seat of the vehicle, besides the middle. The driver, passenger, and backseat riders all engage targets from within the vehicle and then dismount to engage further.

Make sure that each person is proficient on each firearm and continue to rehearse these situations. Eventually, you'll run a multi-stage range where you'll react to ambushes which consist of taking out a roadblock at the front and targets at a close distance on each side of the vehicle; reacting to a pursuit where you pass the targets then stop, dismount, and engage your would-be pursuers; you have an old vehicle filled with targets to mimic a pursuit vehicle and begin engaging it from all sides of your vehicle; stop to let out dismounts while you continue on to engage other targets. The possibilities end with your creativity and these exercises can involve several engagements. The best ranges to run are several building raids that involve driving to each one, dismounting, and entering. Ambush drills and roadblock drills are necessary and should be practiced regularly.

Zero, Fives, Twenty Fives, Two Hundreds

Once you know you're going to stop, you never just hop out. Ambushes can be set to where you get out and trigger an IED. Situations can be set up at meeting points to where you are engaged from several distances as you exit the vehicle. There are several steps that you need to take before jumping out of your covered escape box known as a vehicle.

First, you check Zero meters out. This is the immediate ground to the outside of your vehicle. You check this to assure that you're not stepping onto a landmine or any waiting trap. You also check this to assure that you're not stepping into a hole, uneven terrain, any type of live trap, an animal, or anything that can harm you.

Second, you check five meters out. This is everything within roughly twenty feet of your vehicle to make sure there's no tripwires, waiting IEDs, clearly placed obstacles, or people that could easily engage with pistol or grenade. The five meter point is critical because it's the kill radius of a grenade and grenades are easily made into a variety of drops. Grenades are relatively small compared to a full size IED which has a limitless payload. These small explosions kill everything within five meters, some up to seven or even ten.

Next, you check out to twenty-five meters. This is your close ambush radius where an enemy can wildly spray rounds and effectively hit you. A grenade can be thrown out to thirty-five meters, so this range is also within the critical danger zone when you dismount. An Explosively Formed Penetrator (EFP), a claymore, or directional IED will have nearly maximum effect at this range and will leave you like shredded hamburger. This range is absolutely critical to check thoroughly before dismounting.

Finally, you check out to two hundred meters. This is where spotters, cameraman, IED/EFP triggerman, or shooters hoping to get away will be located. This allows them to engage you from the distance and then "squirt" to a safe location. The two hundred meter gap assures that you won't be maneuvering on them or pursuing them with any result.

These steps are absolutely critical to your safety, but they must be made in a split second. The last thing you want to do is be caught in a vehicle looking around while your enemy maneuvers. Take a quick look back and forth in a zig-zag pattern at these ranges and dismount with your team simultaneously. I know what you're thinking. "How in the hell do we search all that in a second?" Well, we never know either, so we prayed like hell and went with the plan.

Once you dismount, conduct SLLS, commonly called "seals." This is an old acronym that stands for stop, look, listen, and smell. You should have a tactical pause as you exit the vehicle. This allows you to quickly re-enter the vehicle if you need to. Your team leader may quickly make the call to get back in and leave the area instead of staying to fight. Keeping nearby allows you to do this more effectively.

You look around once again with your zeros, fives, twenty-fives, and two hundreds to see if anything has changed since you've become vulnerable. You may also see things that the window glass has distorted. A clear set of actual eyes on everything is key to your situational awareness. You look for geometric shapes, linear paths on the ground, raised or depressed soil, exposed wires, or eyes that meet yours. I could go on for hours on profiling and body language, but you can learn that in depth from other books.

You Listen for any aggressive chatter or awkward silence. You may also be able to hear rapid footsteps, approaching vehicles, enemy radios, the hiss of a fuse, the charging of a rifle, or a keyword being uttered to begin the attack.

You smell the area and what's in the wind. If you smell chemicals, burning fuse, fuel, fruit smells, the smell of nuts, or very hot plastic, this may tell you that an IED is near, a classic fuse has been lit and will soon activate an explosive, you may be standing in strategically placed fuel to burn you alive, nerve agents may be present, or shock tube may have burned the casing of its wire.

These things can be combat determinants of whether to proceed, run like hell, or not to move at all. Getting into the vehicle again can be both good and bad. Good to help from bullets and get away, bad because an IED will turn it into a burning coffin, especially if the charge misfires due to improper compression.

During my first deployment, we had plenty of arguments that ended with the invocation of rank. Every detail was discussed from vehicle speed, spacing between vehicles, and who engages what with what. There's pros and cons to everything. In regular Security Escort Team driving, you are generally far exceeding the speed limit so that no vehicle has an excuse to be anywhere near you. One that gets close is free to engage. In military convoys, slow moving can save lives, especially on harsh terrain with IEDs. Close spacing can assure your enemy cannot divide and conquer but allows a single IED to take you all out. Then there's the aspect of sectors of fire, appropriate weapons, and who can be employed to the greatest strategic advantage. In a world full of hard-dick warfighters, everyone wants to do the shooting and kill the enemy. Planning prevents this from becoming a cluster fuck and still allows enemy killing.

Once you're comfortable in practicing all of this, are a competent mounted/dismounted badass with a vast array of weapons, look into how you can further advance these skills. I recommend attending Personal Security Detail school, learning how to work well in a Security Escort Team, and look into the Guardian Angel method of force protection.

As I've said before, my first appointment was spent on PSD, SET, and Guardian Angel details. We escorted the BMTF to the Pakistan border on a daily basis while on mission cycle. We also served as a chauffeur to everyone above the rank of Lieutenant Colonel who wanted to visit the Pakistan Border's mid-bridge line. We escorted these Birds and Stars up to the Karzai Presidential Billboard, took a lot of selfies, and paraded these men around. The Afghanistan-Pakistan border in the Khyber Pass is absolutely key terrain and unbelievably dangerous. Children with pushcarts routinely cut through our lines, spoke no English, and couldn't be shot. One little bastard had a pushcart full of wires and large black containers. Due to the sensitivity of the area, we would have had to take casualties to justify firing in that civilian-packed walkway. It's one of those times where you have to hope that nothing goes wrong. We even had a man walk up with a wheel barrow with mortar rounds and an artillery shell. Not the casing, the tip.

The more training you have in these environments, the better. There are security contractors all over the nation that are looking for intelligent, skilled individuals who are willing to step into danger to protect someone else. I strongly urge you to seek out these groups and work with them for a couple of years. Their training is priceless, and their job experience is even more so. If you're not into private security, try privatized law enforcement or privatized military. There are groups that employ law enforcement officers to work exclusively for their corporation. This is why I urge you to go through the police academy. That certification opens up a vast range of jobs in both the private and government fields. Privatized law enforcement are commonly used by corporations as a means to have immediate law enforcement response. You'd be a regular security guard, but your credentials give you far superior authority and enable you to make far more money.

Whatever you decide to do, do it knowing that you are the hardest person that anyone has ever tried to kill.

When Things Go Awry

Mistakes happen, snitches are everywhere, alliances fail, and people change. These things can have drastic consequences for teams and can lead to death or worse. Some fights, you just lose and there's nothing you could have done better.   You did everything you could, but the enemy put you in checkmate long before you knew of their new tactic. If we could run and survive forever, there would be no need for the rest of this book. However it happened, you're in enemy custody. Whether they suspected you of something and simply snatched you up for interrogation, busted you with your supplies and are holding you on charges, or they caught you after blaze of hell-fire after you ran out of ammunition, it does not matter. All that matters is that they have you.

You must think of the others in your group. There's a reason that they captured you instead of killing you. They think that you have information, and they desperately need it. They need the information because they genuinely don't know anyone else that's connected or else you would all be in custody. Your job is to Admit to nothing, Deny everything, Assert defenses, and Make counter accusations (ADAM). Your friend ADAM will help you through all sorts of situations. You should remain silent, play stupid, and act as if you have a genuine question as to why you're in custody. Look into their accusations and use logic to talk your way out of it while maintaining your innocence. It is your job to act as if you are cooperating and it is their job to prove you guilty. Since we are in the United States of America, the items you had are legal and common-place. Consistently assert that you're not a member of any group and that you began storing supplies because you saw the nation going through rough times. Act as if you're relieved that the new government is in charge so that your life can get back to normal. The newly installed government will likely recognize this and may have options for you to simply surrender supplies in exchange for your release. If you've lived your cover story, use ADAM, and feign cooperative, they'll likely rule that you're not a threat.

A dedicated enemy believes that they've investigated you, thoroughly done their homework and will present **their facts** to their superiors. Your job through this is to talk to those superiors with a genuine concern of why you're there. Make it sound as if those officers are far over-reaching in their authority, misconstruing the facts, and viewing your actions through a paranoid or over-zealous light. Act as if you are cooperating with the boss, show submissiveness to his authority, and act as if he's the only remedy to the situation. You never want to threaten to go over their head, look at them with contempt, or downplaying their position. If you do this, they may begin to fear you and extrapolate evidence, write it in your file that you threaten them, or are simply too dangerous to release. You can never throw too much smoke.

Prepare To Be Searched And Questioned

The only real way to avoid or evade lawful authority is to adhere to it and jump through the hoops when necessary. If an investigator comes poking around, present your licenses, permits, and whatever other paperwork is needed. Just as you were required to show your driver's license and proof of insurance when stopped in traffic, you're required to show paperwork for certain items you own. Any discrepancies can have serious consequences. No matter how skilled you are, you cannot evade the law for long. Law enforcement have years to build a case on you and years to file for an indictment. They may not even act the first time to catch you committing a crime. Some lay in wait for years.

If they have lawful authority, such as the FBI conducting an investigation into your online purchases, it pays to be honest and explain why you buy things. Should you throw smoke, lie, or skew things, you can be charged with obstruction of justice. Even if everything turns out to be legal, it's still a federal crime to lie to any government officer.

Some of the supplies you buy in general will put you into watch lists with our government due to the fact that over the last 100 years, serial killing has become faddish and shooting at public places has evolved into a highest kill streak award. Don't mind those who come around to investigate. You should be truthful, honest, and welcoming. If you're obeying the law, you have nothing to worry about. That is, as long as the investigator is acting in accordance with the law.

If you have any short barrel rifles, short barrel shotguns, pistols with vertical fore grips, or other items registered to you, you can bet that the Bureau of Alcohol, Tobacco, Firearms and Explosives is going to have a plan in place to assure that the laws are being followed. They often conduct integrity checks. You can own any firearm that you want as long as you file the proper paperwork so it pays in the long run to have your sawed off shotgun, homemade pipe gun, and your homemade ballistic knife registered as manufactured firearms with the proper ATF Form 1; your short barrel, fully automatic, suppressed rifle and your short barrel breaching shotgun should be properly registered using the ATF Form 4. Your grenade launcher, pipe bombs, claymores, rocket launchers, mortar tube, large bore firearms, and everything else can also be registered as Any Other Weapon (AOW) with the ATF. It sounds outlandish but as long as you have the proper licensing and a serial number on each pipe bomb, the ATF has properly signed off and the tax stamp is complete, you legally own those items. Now, I'm not sure how much has changed in firearms legislation over the last few years so check on the ATF website and your local laws for up-to-date information.

Also, have a lawyer establish a gun trust and work closely with them. An experienced lawyer can be a great asset through all of this, and should you ever come into a problem with the government, the lawyer will already know the case throughout and have defenses prepared. Your lawyer will also know what authority you're acting under, what laws are being strictly followed, and how to handle anyone who comes around asking questions.

Accidental invasion of Pakistan - 2014

Controlled DET behind a friend - Torkham 2014

Torkham Border Crossing – your author guarding dirt piles

The priceless Khyber Pass view - Torkham, Afghanistan 2013

OP 5 - Torkham 2013

Torkham 2014

Torkham 2014

Tool bag of the year 2014 - first place: Ryan Taylor

South Kabul 2016

South Kabul 2016

A hand carved rock from a gorgeous Romanian corporal - Kandahar, Afghanistan 2015

King's Palace - Kabul, Afghanistan 2016

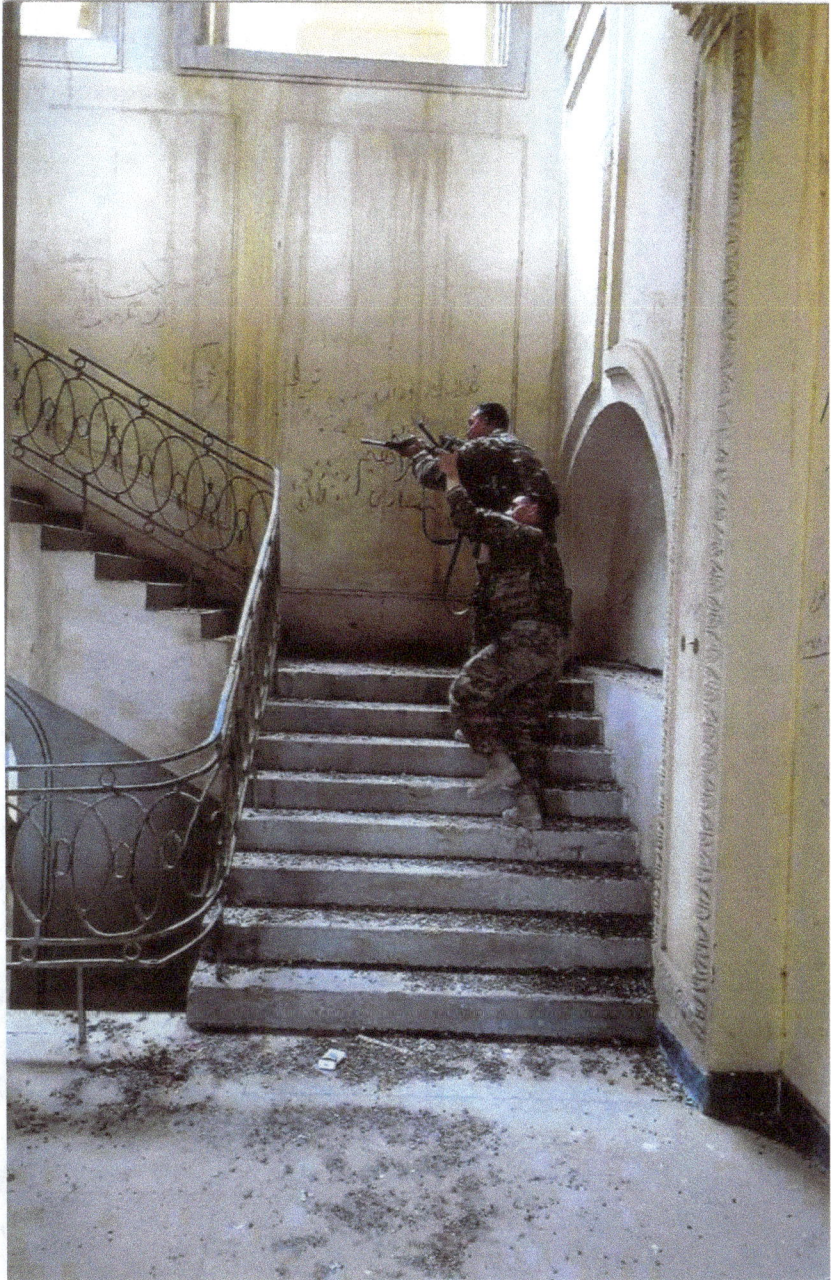

Darul Aman Palace - South Kabul, Afghanistan 2016

Sitting on the Afghan Commandos General's couch

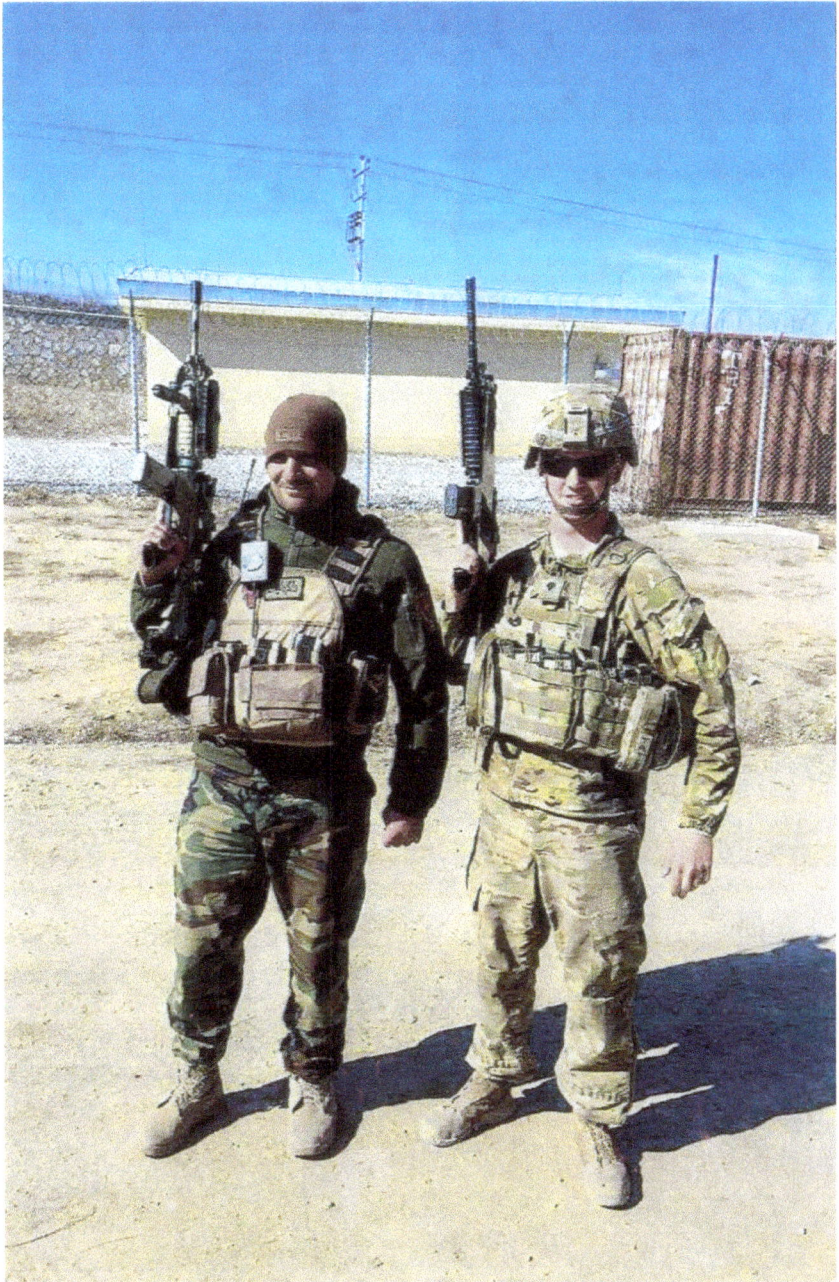

Me and an Afghan Special Forces Operator

The friendly village goat - 2017

OPFOR 2017 - Yes, that's a turtleneck and a collared shirt

Operation Mountain Peak 2017

March 2017 - 15 days of sleeping 1-3 hours a night in the woods, walking all day and doing bullshit swamp missions makes me into this guy. He's an asshole.

I shot 13th overall and our team came in 3rd

Look like everyone else, but be ready to act like no one else

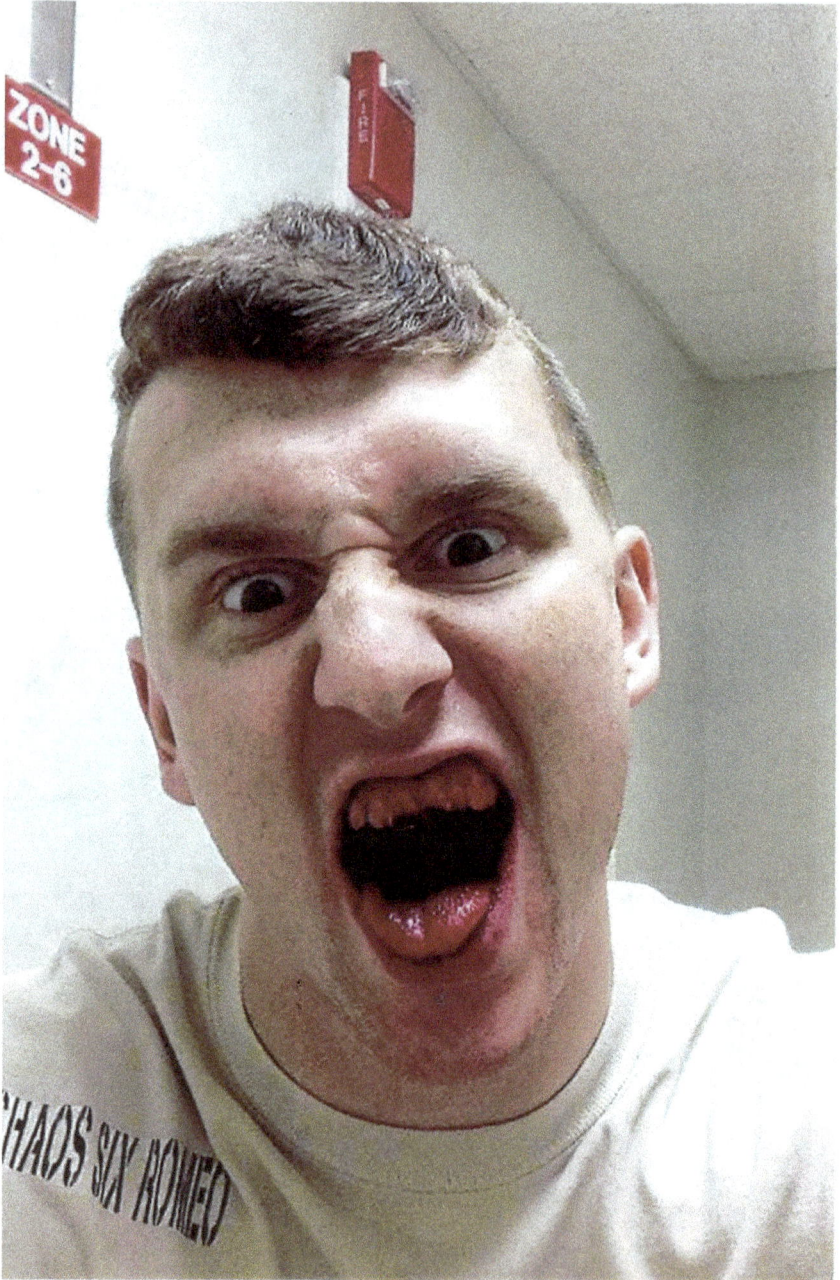

Chaos Six Romeo after a great time. This was right before my second deployment

Me and Josh Clark, who is now deceased. Until Valhalla, hail!

Me and Billy. Used with permission of Billy Jo Waters

My workout partners: Buff, Billy, me, and Raven Burkhow

Chapter 5

Resistance

This is where things get interesting. You've been brought in by an enemy with outlandish claims. It's time to use ADAM to the fullest extent, play your role harder than ever, manipulate, network and do what you need to do in order to remain sane. Much of this starts with the small things that have evolved into principles. Regardless of your political views, you're now neutral and passive. You should act as if you've submitted to the enemy's authority and that you agree that their conduct is lawful. The last thing you want to do is show them that they were right in detaining you. We're going to cover a broad range of topics here and they'll both alert you to what can happen, help you prepare for the worst, and keep you from becoming a mindless drone.

Several principles must be discussed before all this. In any kind of incarcerated environment, the people there with you are all snakes. They'll step on you to get out, make outlandish accusations, and they don't care if you do the rest of your life in that place because of their bullshit. The rats and snitches who provide thorough and reliable information can point the finger at someone and have them removed. The intelligence crew will take their word, write erroneous things in your file, or even throw you in the hole based off of their rat's word. It's a principle not to collaborate or fraternize with the enemy guards but many people will not do this. As the guards are the source of everything from the outside, some contact and conversation is necessary. Whether you're on the enemy's good side or bad side, they're still your enemy. They'll toss a life sentence on you just to make themselves look good on paper, so they're brainless snitches.

First And Foremost

Never use the enemies terms. Your cell is your house, your uniforms are your wardrobe, your bunk is your bed, the mess hall is the restaurant, work details are your career, chow is cuisine, recreation time is recess, the angry guards Uncle Herbert and Aunt Dorothy, the Lieutenant is mom, the captain is dad, the warden is grandpa. Your cell mate is your roommate, the inmates are residents and neighbors, cell blocks are apartment buildings, medical is the clinic, laundry is the laundromat or the dry-cleaners, or the washateria for you southern folks, education is the school, the fences are in the hedges, and the spaces between buildings are the lawn.

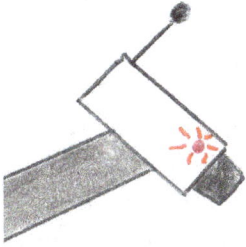

When on
camera,
Be on
camera.

You can become infinitely creative with your terms, and it does wonders for maintaining a semblance of normality while you're stuck there.

Make Sure The Enemy Sees You As A Person

You can appeal to the enemy's emotional triggers, sexuality, and psychological triggers. Some are egotistical and you can earn their respect through noticing what they do. Some are narcissists and you can earn their respect by shaming some of their partners while comparing the two. You can play on a mother's emotions, a father's values, and exploit times that you see any of them become emotionally charged. Find what triggers their humor, anger, happiness, and what they can't stand to see. With all of them, be polite, respectful, stroke their egos, feign stupid and obedient, and study them endlessly.

When On Camera, Be On Camera

Most organized places these days have some sort of surveillance to monitor their prisoners. These protect staff while documenting what each prisoner does. Key things can be reviewed such as hand-offs, conversations, incidents, and who someone's common acquaintances are. You get to paint your own picture for the cameras. While on camera, you must continually be the innocent citizen.

In the feds, there is no self-defense. There's assault, and there's a fight. They expect you, when punched in the face, to put your hands in the air and scream for staff. As unrealistic as it is, it applies constantly. Every altercation, both people are going to be disciplined unless one is a straight bitch. It pays to know these things when going into an incarcerated environment because it can be used to your advantage. Likewise, if an intelligence group is monitoring cameras to watch what you do, they can only report what they personally observe you do. They report without bias, who they see you associate with, what your actions are, and where you go.

In an environment where everyone is a potential snake or a life sentence for you, it pays to get on the enemy's good side. Learn their rank structure and find a good job. Yes, the trash crew provides you a means to collect valuable things and a job in the kitchen allows you to eat what you want, but you should be concerned with your image. Get into a position of trust. The lieutenant's or captain's orderly always has a bad jacket of being a snitch but their word is relied on. If some screw-ball tries to bait you into something stupid, you will be believed. Then, there's tool-room jobs and maintenance jobs that allow you to get near tools and vital supplies. Positions of trust allow you to paint your picture effectively because everyone is watching you. The people you work for, the enemy in each area, and your fellow neighbors. You can "show" your enemy that you can be trusted.

However, if you're serving a lawful sentence, it is better to just do your time. Use these skills to make your time easier and make more money. It is important not to cross a lawful captor as it will add derogatory items to your jacket. The last thing you want is to be an extremely high security risk, this guarantees that you will be housed with the worst people imaginable. You want to show that you need not be watched at all.

Hands On

If you're tortured, bullshit them nonstop. They already have a torture schedule that encompasses twenty-four hours of your day. Your sessions, what will be done, your movement, your sleep time, everything is planned beforehand based on identified physical, mental, and emotional factors that you display. This is precisely why you should feign a cooperative bitch demeanor. Hardasses get things far worse than those who cannot handle it. They'll torture an SF operator far worse than they'll torture the barista from the coffee shop.

Even if you tell them everything, you'll be tortured on schedule. No matter what you give up, they believe that there's far more information to be mined. This is why you need a well-rehearsed cover story beforehand, and you only expose bits and pieces of it as you go. You're already going to endure the full torture program and the possibility that you feign fear at a certain instrument then begin talking, they might not use that instrument. You might forgo a step of your torture schedule before having to get roughed up any further. The longer you hold out, the better you may be. If they have an eight-session schedule for you and you break on three, they might believe that you're giving reliable information. Those who begin spewing bullshit are often tortured more or even beyond schedule. Hold down as much as you can and only give what's necessary, according to the schedule that you've made to release information. No matter what, you are in for the whole program and if they believe there is more, they may have you go through another program. The mind game is not knowing what is ahead of you.

If you don't want to make something up or worry about having to remember the details, tell the truth, about your personal enemies. If there's a drug dealer, human trafficker, or other scumbag near you, you can quickly paint a picture of them being the leader of a terrorist organization or whatever else you'd like to get you off the hook. Ask any drug dealer, the cops will believe anything, and the "leader" is simply the first person not to tell on their next boss.

To really throw them off, give up the name of their officers, captain and above, and try to pin them as the organization leaders. Tell the truth of the operations, just change the players and the pieces of the puzzle will begin to fit. At that point, you'll have officers hiding evidence to cover their boss and it will sow confusion which destroys trust.

Torture isn't just the stereotypical infliction of pain that you see in the movies. Modern torture is devised by master psychologists, elicitors, behavioral experts, profilers, overseen by doctors, and approved by a board of ethics. However, a barbarian enemy who is not acting under law will not observe this and may, in fact, result to heinous methods. Torture can be as brutal as the person inflicting the pain and their imagination is the limits. A thing to be aware of is an inexperienced torturer or one that makes things up on the fly. These types of people often pour on too much and the result is death.

To avoid death, each tactic of modern torture is studied over a long period of time based on which countries employed the method, how long each session is, whether the information given was reliable, and whether a better means is available. Military doctors from all backgrounds review these methods as part of a board to determine what is acceptable, what is effective, and what would be illegal to do. The criteria they review is not up for discussion, but it is effective, and their opinions are then reviewed by several other departments before a method is approved.

In modern interviews, the interviewer often is a behavioral expert, experienced profiler, or an experienced elicitor. Some are cross trained in each field and some interviews have multiple interviewers. Each interviewer is working off of decades of thorough training and experience. They can tell what's reliable, what's not, and when a person is hiding information. Once they deliver their professional opinion that the target is concealing vital information and their methods alone will not work, the fun and excitement begin as the "further methods" team gets together. This team is comprised of a wide variety of staff which range from chemists, doctors, phlebotomists, surgeons, and experienced interviewers. It is a team that fully employs checks and balances to ensure effective means and the extraction of truthful intelligence.

It's important to note that a target might not see the same interrogation technician twice. A thorough schedule is formed that fully encompasses their ability to resist the means, physical health, emotional health, mental health, their exact diet, and amounts of sleep given. The job is to get the information out of a target without causing visible damage. Many of the new methods include intravenous introduction of chemicals which have a variety of effects on the body. They cause mild to absolutely severe pain while the patient is monitored on an EKG. These methods can be started and stopped at will, keep a person under a specific level of pain, and a variety of undesirable bodily functions. Each interrogator is briefed to go into a room and perform a single act on a target. The method, how many times to use it, duration of use, threat of use beforehand, and whether or not to threaten it afterward are all discussed previously.

Should you ever be subjected to this, you'd better have a plan, and it helps to practice mindfulness. Knowing that it can't last forever, the people inflicting the pain are trained in this and have done far worse, they can't let you die, and they often won't leave a mark as it will reflect poorly on their government. They'll play games to make you mentally hurt yourself by believing that they really are idiots who might kill you by accident. This sort of thing is just the beginning. Pay attention to who is who, who comes back, and who prefers which instruments. Some don't have the stomach for this sort of thing, but you'll never know. Their oversight has all of this knowledge and builds schedules that also will not personally harm their employees. Prevention of psychological damage and PTSD of their interrogators is their first priority. You're the second.

The following are some interrogation techniques that have been used in recent history. Some of these are quite effective while others are intended to be purely mind games. Some cause permanent psychological damage, physical damage, and lead to several forms of illness.

As a means to get information out of you, governments throughout the last century have become creative and adept in doing so.

The Methods They've Used

1. **Physical Infliction of Pain**- This involves beatings with objects, closed fist punches, kicking, clubbing, and tossing a person around the room.
2. **No More Peace at Night**- They'll wake you up at all hours of the night and initiate their chosen game cycle. Sleepy, groggy, half focused people will often talk simply to go back to bed.
3. **Persuasion**- This involves the use of friendly staff. Every desk clerk and non-interrogation personnel you come across will have stories of the horrors they've seen, how strong you are for making it that far, and that by simply talking, you can make it all stop. They make the enemy sound like a reasonable person with good intentions. Some of them may even offer you money, a relationship when you get out, or say they can guarantee that you'll get better treatment.
4. **Personality Contrast**- This is the old good cop-bad cop routine where one comes in wild and the other acts as if he actually cares. There's calculated conflict between the two in order to make you fear one and trust the other.
5. **Humiliation**- This works well on both males and females. They'll strip you naked in front of the opposite sex and have you on display. Their people know the routine so they utter degrading comments as they pass, openly laugh at you, tell you that you're misshapen, and anything else they can think of to degrade you. They have their staff act disgusted towards you.
6. **Extreme Confusion**- This has a wide variety of tricks. They may have you shackled to your bunk and a guard will randomly come in and take a shit in your toilet or sink while staring at you. A female may enter the interrogation room, undress fully then paint all her nails and randomly leave without saying a word. Older officers who should be experienced may come in and address you as a different name as if they had the wrong packet, get pissed, and storm out. The possibilities of throwing you off are endless.
7. **Promises, Intimidation, and Enticement (PIE)**- They'll threaten to send you to the worst place imaginable only it doesn't exist. Once you get there, they threaten you with an ever more ominous place. It's an endless cycle. On the contrary, they'll promise

to send you to the best place where it's essentially a college dorm setting with conjugal visits for the duration of your stay. Both are absolute bullshit; you're going to where they have bed space.

8. **Deception**- They'll make you think that your friends, spouse, and children have turned on you. They'll tell you that your family and friends have already told them everything and your only way out is to confess. They'll have loud conversations in the hall about case matters or joke about having sex with your spouse, just to see your reaction on camera. They'll make it sound like they've already been questioning your spouse in a different room and that they know everything. Be aware of this shit.

9. **Playing On Your Affections**- They'll threaten to take your kids, send your spouse to the worst camp imaginable, threaten to rape your spouse, tell you that your wife will be put to work in a brothel, anything to get you talking. They'll tell you that you're going to be known as a traitor and you'll be killed where they're sending you.

10. **Sound Games**- Remember this from home defense? Same principle. They'll have intensely loud music playing at all times of night, scratch nails on a chalkboard and play the recording over and over again, they'll sound a train horn every six minutes, or let microphone feedback play over the speakers for a few hours.

11. **Tickling**- This it's not your regular idea of tickling. Have you ever had a thorough coronavirus test? Now, imagine that same feeling but for several minutes at a time with bird feathers, pipe cleaners, hay, straw, and whatever else they think would work.

12. **Minute Pain Infliction**- They'll burn you with cigarettes, lighters, meticulously open different sizes of needles to drive into you, drop a scalpel into your leg from varying heights, and get creative with and awl.

13. **Light Effects**- They'll toss you into a plexiglass box that's surrounded by mirrors. The walls, ceiling, and floors will have mirrors a few inches away. A stadium light is your new roof. They'll leave you like this for days on end just to mess with your sleeping schedule. The bright lights will strain your eyes and your skin will dry out. The light box also keeps the heat in, so it won't drop below 90 degrees the whole time you're in there.

14. **The Just-For-Fun Games**- They'll rush you no matter where you're going just to leave you in a holding cell for hours. They'll come into each of them screaming to hurry up and then simply move you to a different holding cell for a few more hours. They may do this for several days before you even get to an interviewer. They'll issue you a few different uniforms and then have you run back to change it depending on where you're going. They might move you from five or six waiting rooms before ever actually getting to an appointment. Some may even come into the room screaming at you for no reason and simply leave. By the time you get to interrogation, you'll be grateful that the constant moving is over.

15. **The Disciplinary Box**- A plywood box that's custom built to give you two inches of movement on each side. You'll be in this box whenever they're pissed off, whenever you've misbehaved, or at least when they tell you you've misbehaved, and for any other reason they can think of. Information not thorough enough? The box with you! Also, the person who ordered you in is the only person with the authority to let you out. So if you went in on Friday and Mr. X won't be back until Monday, you'd better be good at eating through the small, hinged feeding flap.

16. **Sit**- You'll sit at the very edge of your chair only. If they allow you to sit regularly, the chair will be roughly a foot or so too tall and will have no back. The seat will also be the size of a computer keyboard. Another horrible seat is a four-inch pole, two-inch pole, and the one-inch pole that they have running across the room, roughly four feet from the wall. Unless you know how to sit on this, you are in for a real treat. Each room will have a different sized pole and you'll be "permitted" to sit.

17. **Kneel**- Ever wonder why every room so far has had rugged wood floors even though it's a concrete building, seemingly always full of gravel? Well, now you know. You'll be kneeling at attention for long periods of time. This isn't a nice kneel, it's a stress position where you remain fully erect as if at attention and the weight of your body is directly over your knees.

18. **Stand**- You'll be grateful to be able to stand, despite having no shoes. However, you will be left at parade rest for hours on end. This plays hell with your back and shoulders. Every guard that

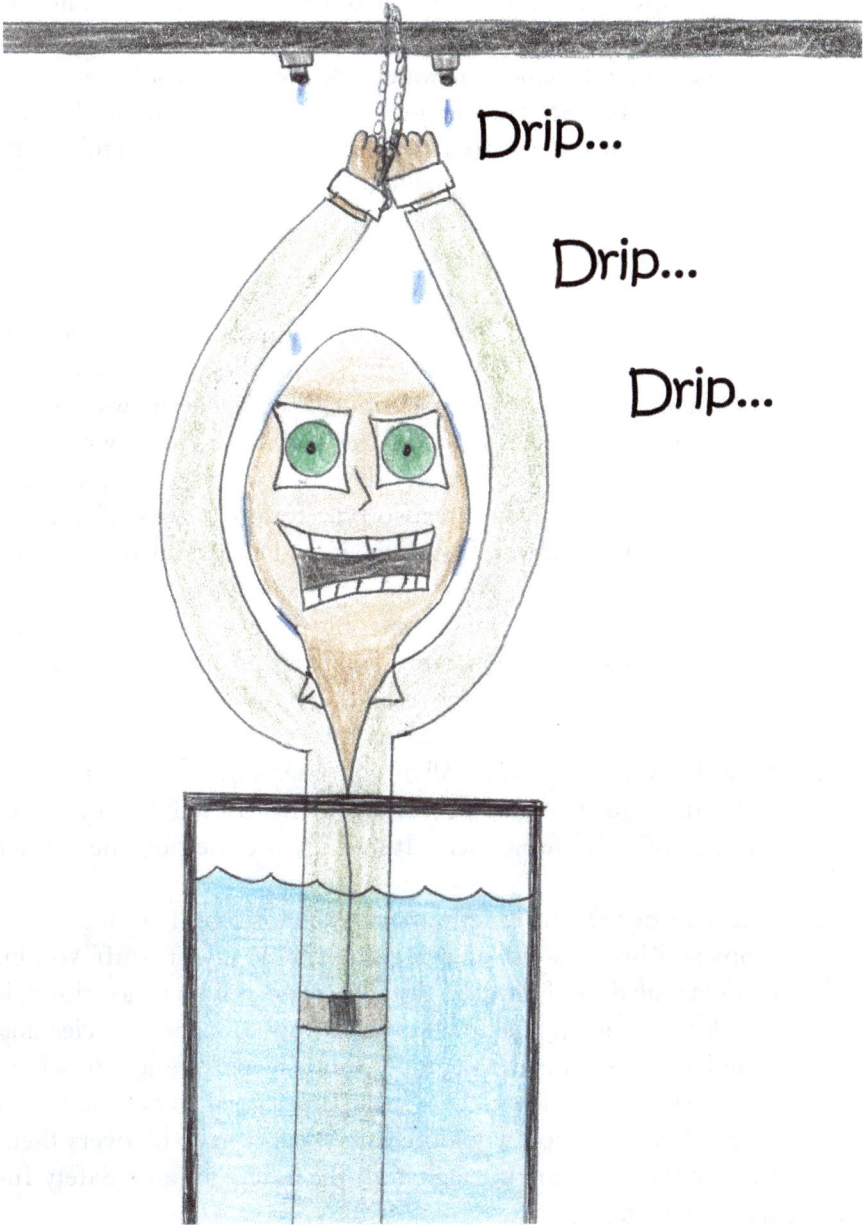

passes on their rounds will alternate you between parade rest and attention. The position of attention is a huge relief. Each guard also knows which position he's supposed to have you in and if you think you can relax to attention, he will catch you.

19. **A Fox Hole**- There's a method of boring a four-foot-wide hole in the ground that's ten feet deep. You'll be placed in this, fed from a bucket, and only enjoy the water that they spray you with. Minus the urine and defecation that you'll leave on the ground. This also never dries out and is extremely cold. They generally do this in the basement so that you're actually dug into the permafrost. Don't think about trying to bore the hole out further, it's thin concrete but it's concrete, nonetheless.

20. **Water Deprivation**- Ever had a bag of chips for your three daily meals? Well, you're going to. The only water you will have is what they throw onto you. Generally, you'll be in a dry cell which consists of a slightly risen steel floor, almost like the walls of an industrial dryer. This is made so they can hose you down whenever they feel like it. You won't die since your skin will soak up water. Rumor has it, you can absorb up to four glasses of water in a twenty minute shower. Look this up and check out some of the literature on it.

21. **Sleep Deprivation**- They'll not only have you interrogated at night, they will move you every two hours from block to block. They make sure that the move takes twenty to thirty minutes to complete, then they have to count you.

22. **Solid Food Deprivation**- All of your meals will consist of blended beans, vegetables, and protein powder. It's a fully balanced diet but lack of solid food sucks. It's a measure used on the weaker minded folks.

23. **The Closet**- This is exactly what it sounds like. They'll take the mops and brooms out of a regular hallway closet, stuff you in, and lock the door. However, this closet was not built as a closet, it was designed as a punishment cell and only contained the cleaning supplies so as to further degrade you. It's small enough to where you can't sit or lie down. This space is designed so no one would ever believe a person would be housed in it. It also covers them if their leaders come through with the Sanitation and Safety Inspection List.

24. **Many Interrogators**- You may go through a ridiculous amount of interrogators. Most of the time, they're the receptionist, janitor, and other desk jockeys that pose as other agencies or departments. You may go through fifty interrogators and never see the same one twice, this means you'll have to tell your full story over and over again. Also, since they claim to be from different departments or agencies entirely, "they don't conduct interagency communications." It's a game to keep you regurgitating the information.

25. **Infested Housing**- They'll have you in an ant, roach, mouse, rat, mole, fly, gnat, and lizard infested area of the compound for a while. This area is intended to cause restlessness, discomfort, fear, and mild irritation. None of these pests are actually harmful and they're normally bred in the camp. Doctors are also nearby in the event that a subject has an allergic reaction to the venom. Poisonous or venomous snakes and spiders are generally not used. However, don't be surprised if a sidewinder or cobra slither in, they're no longer able to kill you but they're intimidating and still bite. A less organized enemy may use the real thing.

26. **Punishment Cell**- The punishment cell comes in two flavors, Hot and Cold. The hot one generally is a well-insulated capsule where they heat the place to a controlled temperature. This can also be an outdoor wood shack with a low tin roof design to cook you. Water rations are limited, and you'll be too hot to eat. The temperature in these fluctuate between one hundred to one hundred thirty degrees. The cold cell is a concrete cell that is also controlled temperature. The walls are kept sweating and the temperature inside fluctuates between fifty to sixty degrees. Your water rations remain the same, but they cut your food rations.

27. **The Special Hole**- There's a two-foot wide by two-and-a-half foot deep hole in a concrete wall. They close you in using a heavy steel mesh door. Strategically above you is a water pipe where they can vary the speed of the trickle. Generally one drop every three to fifteen seconds. This frozen chamber will drive you mad.

28. **Food Deprivation**- This is where they've calculated your resting metabolic rate and they'll give you roughly half of that. Every week you spend in calorie deficit, you'll get one balanced meal to make sure that you have the proper nutrients to stay alive, just not

the calories to replace what you're losing. They keep your meals limited to a single serving bag of chips, a single chocolate bar, a horrible and stale snack cake, or a plain hotdog. Meanwhile, they'll house you near the kitchen so you can smell all of the baked goods and fried food provided to their guards. Anytime you're housed elsewhere, you'll be able to fully view a guard eating a full meal, munching away on good snacks, or simply throwing whole plates of food away in front of you. This is done as a mind game.

29. **No Mark Beatings**- They'll beat you with hoses, punch you through books, use sandbags, beat you with sacks of putty, boxing gloves, open hand slaps, high pressure water, hurling your meal at you, or slamming you into walls from a few inches away.

30. **Straight Jackets**- They'll leave you in a straight jacket for days just to watch you urinate and defecate on yourself. They'll leave you like this for days on end and may even combine this tactic with their infestation cell.

31. **The Leg Wrap**- This is a means of physical restraint that is like a tiny hook and loop sleeping bag. It's used to fasten your legs tightly together and it has several carrying handles with a carabiner on the back to keep your hands shackled in place.

32. **The Bridle**- They'll leave you with an actual bridle in which makes everything significantly more stressful. This can be a steel bar, ball gag, dental wedges, or simply tying a cloth into your mouth. This restricts eating, drinking, breathing, and can even activate your gag reflex constantly.

33. **The Arm Deep Pool**- They'll have your feet tied to a pole at the side of this pool and they'll slowly fill it until your arms are fully stretched out. You're stuck in the front-leaning rest, and you are there until further notice. They'll change the level of the water constantly, so you'll be out of it wondering why you're still locked out and other times they'll raise it to submerge you. You will collapse from exhaustion several times before they pull you out. If you look closely, you'll notice the post at your feet is outside of another pole so that it swings like a hinge. If you look closely, you'll also notice that they have a means to mechanically raise your body out of the water once you go unconscious.

34. **Time Deprivation**- No matter what, they deprive you of time. You will never see a clock, watch, or calendar. This helps add to

the stress since you can't measure how long each session lasts, know when the next is about to start, and when anything else will be. You'll begin to believe that they have the power to do this to you for all of eternity.

35. **The Petty Criminal**- You'll see them haul in a petty criminal just to see what he complains of. Generally, they snitch unintentionally. "How can you bring me in for this when you have people out there doing . . ." They deflect attention from them by complaining of what others are doing. This provides a clear picture for their captors of who will cooperate and who is still out there. These people generally give up names and addresses.

36. **Rape and Fear of It**- Equally effective against male and female detainees, the fear of being raped will often get people to talk. Whether it be sexual abuse at the hands of your captors or them threatening to toss you into a wrong housing area that's filled with heinous sex criminals, the fear gets people to cooperate. Rape is seen as the ultimate degradation for both men and women in modern society. Anytime men have absolute power over female population, sexual abuse will happen if they are not closely monitored.

37. **Elicitation**- The clever tactic of getting you to tell them what they want to know. The clever enemy knows how to breakdown your psychological and emotional defenses and can easily make you want to talk to them. They exploit your need to correct errors in records, your need to justify actions, and get inside of your mind. Like an experienced body language expert, these people know how to read you and what questions to ask to make you stumble.

38. **Wait**- When someone gets picked up, they generally share their stories with other inmates of how the incident happened, how the enemy messed up or violated their rights, and will also need to be cleared through peers. This process is almost required amongst inmate populations. You let them know who you are, that you didn't tell on your partners, and that you're not a sex offender. Populations everywhere want to know who is living with them and inmates are no different. By simple holding cell monitoring, the enemy can find out nearly every detail, even some that they didn't know before. People will also be asking questions to see if

your story checks out, make sure that you're not an undercover enemy, and that you're not secretly a sex offender. Rats are everywhere so watch your tongue. By frying you for the court, they may walk free.

39. **Fake Evidence and Statements**- The enemy may act like they have you nailed when they are clearly fishing you for details. They may have nothing or make wild accusations waiting for you to deny only part of the record. " Everyone else already told me what happened, I've got the full record right here. This is your time to make sure that you only get charged with what you did, because right now, it sounds like you were the leader." Sounds like a sad drug detective with no case? This is the line they often use to ensure cooperation.

40. **Seizure of Assets**- They will threaten to take everything from you. House, vehicle, personal effects, you name it. They will do this regardless of your cooperation so it's best to tell them to piss off. Besides, where you're going, if they really have you, you won't care much about free world property. More so when the enemy hands out life sentences for small infractions or word of mouth convictions.

These are some of the more common tactics and methods used in information extraction over the last century or so. I stopped at forty because there's far too much to list and anything else may constitute classified information. "I've only shared what is publicly available through diligent research on the subject, which is where I learned this."

So when you've already had a rough life avoiding the enemy and trying to support your family and your group, you get to endure these methods. Whether you were turned in by a snitch for the million reasons they can come up with, made a fatal slip such as a questionable purchase, or they flat out captured you in a gunfight, you've got these things to look forward to.

It is important to know what you may be subject to beforehand, this way you can mentally prepare yourself and you'll be thinking "Thank Odin that they didn't use the bamboo slivers, electric shock, bamboo water cage, fake executions, cat-o-nine tails, centrifugal roller torture, the hot bucket rat, finger nail and tooth extraction, defacing surgeries performed with a hunting knife, castration, female genital mutilation, try all of this on my family in front of me, or kick my dog."

Too graphic? Good. Maybe you will remember the fact that there are absolute sadists out there who enjoy doing these things to people and you're just as vulnerable as anyone else in the world. All it takes for them to capture you and your family is a well-placed nitrous tank or a tranquilizer dart. Then, the world as you know it went from post apocalypse hell to Ted Bundy's Playground. Keep yourself and your family safe and recognize that even a fake friend can lead to your demise.

When you've had enough of the torture camp, perhaps you should think of getting out of it. . . Here we go!

Chapter 6

Slippery Otter

So, you're stuck in some sort of confinement by an enemy. Clearly, you're of some value to them since they haven't killed you yet or executed you after running your name through their database. Now, what in the hell do you do in order to return to the fight, return to your loved ones, and continue to fight for the homeland? Yes you guessed it. You get out of confinement. It's noteworthy to add that if you're lawfully confined, the fastest way out is to simply complete your lawful sentence. Nothing in this section will apply to lawful detention inside the United States. This chapter serves the sole purpose of showing you how to slip the custody of terrorists, invading armies, or anyone else who has kidnapped you. Should you try this kind of thing in the United States, either federal prison or in a state prison, it will quickly fail due to the procedures in place. Should you ever actually see the inside of a lawful institution, the construction, staff training, and secret squirrel shit that's hidden from you will quickly foil your plans. It's also noteworthy that federal agents routinely work in federal prisons as inmates to takedown notorious criminals, rogue staff, and potential threats that are developing. So, you not only have to worry about the plethora of snitches, you may in fact be conversing with a federal agent. Only the warden is notified of the agents identities and these people prosecute whatever comes across their nose indiscriminately.

No matter what, avoid using the E word. As you can clearly tell what this chapter is about, you should note the change in name. In most combat scenarios, war fighters are bound by the United States Code of Conduct. Take a look at this now and read each article carefully. This details what you, too, will need to do in order to flee the enemy. The reason you never use the E word is because it draws attention. Even the enemy may recognize this word in English and become aware of your unscheduled release.

Education

First and foremost, education is the key. Your job is to quickly learn the language of your invader. You should monitor foreign relations to better prepare yourself and know which language books to keep around. You can never be too educated so I recommend that you have a stable base established in French, Russian, German, Spanish, and Italian. You'll quickly notice that French, Spanish, and Italian have glaring similarities.

Once you learn one, you get a grasp on the others automatically. As Germany is another of our allies, it may come in handy to know when talking with fellow NATO troops. In Kabul, we had the Germans roll up to our base and ask to use our airfield. We had no German interpreter, and they had no English interpreter. Over there, we worked closely with the Italians, Romanians, Australians, Royal troops, the Polish, and the Germans. ROMSOF and POLSOF are incredible war fighters. Russian is a key language due to its popularity and status as one of the world powers that could actually invade. There's not much of a chance at an invading Arab force but terrorists do capture people abroad. Wherever you're planning on traveling, know the language of the host nation and the language of any radical groups that plagued the area. Despite what you've seen in Ukraine, they can be a competent enemy. With a clear understanding of those languages, you can quickly learn other similar languages.

Don't be like me on my first deployment. I began to learn Arabic to prepare myself for Afghanistan. I got here and quickly learned that they speak Pashto, Dari, Farsi, and some Hindu. They write with the Arabic alphabet.

Knowledge of their language and how to read it properly will come in handy when communicating, though you never let the enemy know that you know the language, and reading their maps, manuals and orders that you may be able to glance at. The more fluent you are, the better you'll be when it comes time to apply the skill.

Learn Them, Fluently

Your key to freedom is studying them nonstop. You should be able to identify your enemy by name at first glance. The way they wear their uniform, the way they walk, their mannerisms, their tics, and other factors that only they exhibit. You'll know them by footsteps, their voice, their silhouette, and where they stand while on shift. Believe it or not, everyone has a specific place they like to stand in a tower, a special place to park while in a vehicle, a special angle they park at, a unique speed they drive at, and several other things that you'll pick up through diligent observation. You'll learn what they like, what they don't like, political affiliations, and how dedicated they are to their job. Some will simply do their shift and go home whereas others will do thorough searches, harass you to check your integrity, and even turn in other staff for misconduct. Take mental notes of all this as it can lead you to discover which staff are their enemies. You may be able to convince one of their enemies to allow you to violate a major rule so as to make Mr. Thorough look bad. Anytime that someone can mess with an enemy and see them held responsible, you are then in a position of power. Learn what your enemy smokes, what they chew, what music they like, and what they do on weekends. This helps them see you as a person, shows them that you have a genuine concern for their well-being, and that you have similarities. These things quickly lead to a rapport.

Make it a point to learn who is on whose shift, how they rotate shifts, how often they patrol, how attentive they are, the weapons they carry, and their level of discipline. By knowing who is on shift, you can coordinate certain things to be done on the lazy guy's shift, the inattentive guy's shift, and avoid the hardass' shift. By knowing their patrol times, you know how long you have to perform a job before you have to be long gone. By knowing each guard's attentiveness level, you can determine how much they will notice, whether or not they'll hear certain noises, or even whether or not they will respond to certain things. By knowing the weapons they carry and how many each man carries, you know the level of resistance to expect from them. Whether it's being bear maced, tazed, or shot, you know what their capability is against you. It also pays to know that a man with a sniper rifle is almost no good in close quarters. A shotgun cannot punch out past a football field unless they're a slug master. A pistol is inaccurate, but the rounds are still effective out to a few hundred meters. There are, however, people who can routinely land shots on a three hundred meter range with their pistol. This is why it pays to know who you are up against. Would you rather be shot by a trained marksman or by a shaking, scared desk jockey? By knowing their level of discipline, you can determine whether or not they're actually doing their job while on duty versus surfing online videos or watching porn on shift. Each has their applications.

The good ones that do their job can be quickly gassed up and are sure to follow procedure. Procedure can be both good and bad. Good in that it looks organized, bad in that it's incredibly slow and stupid, generally requiring several pieces operating in unison. The inattentive ones provide you the opportunity to work without interference for hours on end, often for their whole shift. If you know a hardass is on shift, you can throw a wrench into operations by the smallest infractions. If you know that they are going to run across the compound due to improper footwear, you have a crew member wear the wrong thing. As super-douche brainlessly takes off on the offending shoes like a scud missile, you can easily pass off your hacksaw blades, knives, nylon cutting string, the ammunition you've gathered and the extra magazines without worrying about the interference. As I've said before, those who know don't care and those who care don't know. The strictest guards compromise security in order to feel like a boss over some dumb shit. Use this.

By simply watching them watching you, you can learn their whole operations system from how they respond to emergencies, suspected escape attempts, friendly rescue operations, injured staff, and medical emergencies. You know which duties they have to do by watching the new guys. Then, you can clearly see what the "experienced" ones overlook due to their "earned laziness." You learn the times that they have to check in, what pattern they report in, and how they switch shifts. You will also see whether or not they go straight home or whether they have a final accountability formation, face to face with their shift leader, or leave in a certain order.

Back in Lafayette, Louisiana, I used my insomnia to my benefit to learn the patrol rounds, what gets searched at night, how thoroughly things get searched, when their shift changes are, who carries the main keys, when the sergeants came around, which ones joked around, which ones were prior military, and I established a baseline for what their policy looked like. This helped me discern which staff I could play around with, which ones were in a position of authority, and who not to mess with.

This one time, they came through for a massive shake down and I had my knife on me. I tossed my extra into the toilet and poured my coffee into it, I had a map of the jail hanging on the wall that I turned into a shopping mall blueprint, and we were all rushed out of the dorm. They came in deep with pepperball guns, bear mace, shields, and an AR with a less-lethal upper. We were all sat on one side of an empty unit and would go in groups of three to be searched then placed on the other side. A hardass, still in his Marine Corps issued boots, stood in the center with the pepperball gun. I was one of the last people left on the one side and I simply walked right past the dude. All that time he stood there, watching attentively, he forgot the rotation. I walked right past him and sat in the "already searched" area. The deputies upstairs doing the searches asked, "anyone left?" Not even they knew what was going on and Mr. Pepperball hardass was too busy flexing to see me walk past. His back was to a wall, and I passed right in front of him, across an open dorm. My fellow inmates knew it, and some burst out laughing, then being told by a hardass to "shut the hell up during the search process!" When I returned to the dorm, my second knife was still in the coffee filled toilet and the map of the jail was still on the wall. This is a perfect example of how the most trained dude in the area out of bravado and ego, overlooked major security issues.

Everyone Is A Mask

No matter where you go, you have the several personality types all rolled into different shifts. Knowing who you're working with will determine what you can get away with. Everyone wears the mask of professionalism but there's a few underlying issues that cannot be hidden. Let's go over some:

The Clown- They can be seen playing during work, they joke nonstop, and are usually preoccupied while on duty. You can break their professional walls by showing similar humor.

The Lazy/Not Caring- This is the "I've earned my right to be lazy" guy. These are the kinds of people who could know where a dangerous weapon or serious contraband is, and they won't care enough to find it. They simply don't want the paperwork associated with it, so they knowingly overlook serious issues.

The Dumb- These guys can care about their job more than anyone else but are too dumb to do things right. They don't know how to search a person, they don't know where to look in a building, and they don't know where to look in a shakedown.

The Hardass- The One that can be seen storming across the place to fix a small infraction and while distracted, not see the real things going on behind the scenes.

The Cool Guy- The cool guy is often desperate for companionship, so much so that they allow their impartiality to be brought into question. These are the guys that might as well be inmates.

The Crooked One- These are the guys that are clearly compromised and are working for the inmates in some context. Whether doing backgrounds for people, bringing in tobacco, drugs, tools, phones, or anything else you are not supposed to have, they'll turn on you the second they get caught. These fools are also stuck in a bind with the inmates, who have leverage over the idiot the moment they dropped the first package.

The Boss- The One that knows all the right answers and his authority cannot be questioned, even if the book answer is clearly contrary. They are overbearing to their coworkers, and you can generally get their peers to rebel against them.

Once you get a feel for who is who, study them intently. Some groups have two or four teams that work twelve-hour shifts. Over a course of two days, you'll have A shift, B shift, C shift, D shift. Every quarter they may switch from AB, CD to BA, DC to change from night shift to day shift, or another rotation entirely. By learning this, you learn who fits in where. If you learn that each letter is a different platoon, you know who closely associates with who. You'll generally know who is on what shift based on their call sign. Some groups work six or eight hour shifts so you might get the full staff working within a twenty-four hour period or over the course of two days. The schedules can alternate in almost any fashion, so it pays to know who is where. Where someone's team is, there are the partners. Weekends and holidays are always subject to change. Some people want overtime and others want time off. The weekends are also not just Saturday and Sunday. The days off will normally vary by shift assignment and rotate with each quarter.

Watch How They Change Shifts

Does the relief show up and take over before someone leaves or does the guard leave? If the guard leaves, you can monopolize. The same goes for the guard's bathroom time. Do they simply leave the post momentarily to the relieve themselves? These things can be critical determinants of how your actions need to be changed and what your plan needs to entail.

At the end of shift, do they check in face to face with their superior, have a release formation, or do they just walk out? If they don't have to check in, no one will notice if you garrote the outgoing shift member.

Do they bring their weapons home, or do they have a dedicated Armory? Knowing this can come in handy if they have a barracks. You can steal weapons while they're in the shower and leadership will remove them over this, believing that they left the weapon at a guard post.

Do they conduct radio checks with each shift change? If not, you may be able to smoke the outgoing shift and then the newly posted guard, maintaining operational safety until the next radio check.

Watch For Their New Trainees And Anyone With A Low Rank

Generally, the leaders will follow the standard exactly as written to show the new people what right looks like. You can overhear key security information, the order of radio checks, call signs, challenge and pass-word, and even that their relief is going to be late. Things like this can be monopolized on.

Bond

No matter who it is, show compassion for them. Make them see you as a person and try to bond with them. By being friendly and talkative, you may be able to have them let their guard down. Ask them for a ciga-rette or a dip of tobacco, talk about what you like to smoke or chew. With men, chewing the same brand of tobacco, smoking the same brand of cigarette, and drinking the same brand of beer show similarities that are subconsciously comforting. People are more comfortable with similar peers. As the saying goes "Birds of a feather flock together."

Ask them for food, water, blankets, hygiene supplies, let them know that you're a person and that you care about your comfort. Simple ges-tures such as these can show good faith on their part, and it builds a bond. If you can make them see you as a person, you can hopefully make your time less rough, perhaps exchange favors, and maybe see that you have a common enemy. By regurgitating the enemy doctrine, you can show them that you agree with why they are there. A like-minded man is not seen as a threat since they believe in the same cause.

Monitor The Posture

Pay attention to how each one handles and carries their weapon. If they don't have a sling on their weapon, you have the possibility of wres-tling it away from them. If they have a sling, the weapon will not easily slip off of their body so you will have to assure that you take them com-pletely out before you try to gain control of it

Slings generally assure that a rifle cannot be turned back around on its user and assures that the weapon stays attached to the user. However, the sling can be a downfall.

If your enemy leaves the rifle dangling on a sling or even better, back slung, you can monopolize on this. The fore end of a rifle is great leverage when strangling someone and can be used to crush their trachea. Similar to the Full Nelson choke, a rifle adds maximum effect to the technique. The sling can also be used for strangulation, should you be able to gain the advantage on your enemy. An enemy who has a firm grip on his rifle and his sling properly used is your huckleberry. Don't mess with him, he's looking to use it.

Whether it's dangling or back slung, it's not in their hands which is the only thing you need to know. With pistols, a lanyard looks ridiculous so many will not use it. It also adds the risk of getting snagged on things as they pass. However, it keeps the weapon effectively tied to their body. Most pistol lanyards will break away at twenty pounds. The sole purpose of a lanyard is to prevent the weapon from being lost if it falls out, it's not made to survive two men having a wrestling match over a pistol. Should you gain control of the weapon, you should know how lanyards are attached to the user. Most are hook and loop fastener, some are key rings, others are actually tied around the belt securely.

Beware The Body Alarm

Whenever you consider taking down an enemy, make sure you take a look at their radio. Some makes and models have a body alarm feature that's activated by manually pressing and orange button on the radio. Several models have more than one button, some are not colored at all, and others have an additional tilt feature. There are several radios that automatically transmit at the onset of loud noises, such as yelling. Once things get too loud, the GPS flag shows in a control center and they monitor the situation to determine whether further assistance is needed.

Should you decide to monopolize on the enemy, beware the radio chirp. If the radio turns into an angry bird, their body alarm will activate within seconds if the radio is not returned to vertical. You can take out an enemy and keep the radio vertical to assure that you can continue with others. Just be cognizant that if a body alarm activates, the radio is essentially a brick until a control center reactivates it. This prevents the distress call from being heard by a belligerent.

As with anything, there are ways to prevent manual activation of the radio's body alarm feature. If the user is unconscious or does not have use of their fingers, they generally cannot activate the feature. The best way to assure success is to gain control of the radio itself. The only downfall of this is the body alarm button on the hand mic, should your enemy be using one. If you grab the radio and take off with it, their control of the hand mic allows them to keep in contact with the radio and activate their body alarm without issue. A hand mic cord is not a lanyard, it won't come apart with twenty pounds of force.

Use Of Force

Your enemy has a lot of tools at their disposal, ranging from less lethal all the way to people obliterators. A reason to know the enemy's language is so that you can research their manuals before they invade and learn their procedures. Most organizations have a use of force policy that is public information and clearly list the criteria necessary to use force. You can do with this what you wish.

A downfall of long guns is that they require enough room to level out. The target must be in front of the barrel for it to be effectively used, otherwise a discharge poses an unnecessary danger. By gaining control of a firearm, you can assure you won't be shot by it. If they have a tight sling on or are a skilled gunslinger, their weapon does them no good when it's sandwiched to their body by yours, especially if you're cutting their throat on the initial contact. Any means to assure that the barrel is not pointed at you will guarantee your safety against that weapon.

Pistols are good for close quarters combat. The rounds are large, can be fired in rapid succession, and the close proximity almost guarantees a target hit. However, pistols are the easiest to disarm someone of. Consult the twenty-one foot rule used by law enforcement. Another downfall of pistols is that it adds leverage to any wrist manipulation that is employed against the user. The barrel of a pistol is like a ratchet handle for the arm.

Should you be confronted by the hardass who sports hard-knuckle gloves and carries a knife, don't engage him. The hard knuckle gloves are a major force multiplier, and a knife is one of the hardest things to fight. In a knife fight, there are no winners, just less dead. Any attempt to disarm a knife wielding individual will likely result in severe bodily injury. If the person is a trained knife fighter, you'll be carved to pieces as if you just boxed a blender.

Weapons

Let's assume that you are of similar stature to myself. Under six feet tall and under two-hundred pounds. You need a force multiplier, and you need it badly.

Firearms are great but one shot will have the entire place crawling on you. If you've ever tossed a sugar cube into an ant hill, you know what a swarm looks like, and this is the effect that a firearm discharge will bring you.

If it's not realistic to gain control of an enemy's weapon, you'll have to improvise. For this reason, any opportunity that you can get to work in a metal shop, maintenance shop, or network with those who do, you should immediately seize it. The best knives require a grinder, heat treatment, and a good quench. After that, handles are easily made with wrapped cordage, homemade micarta, or simply tightly wound rag. Steel is great, stainless won't set off metal detectors, plexiglass is wonderful, aluminum likes to bend and won't hold an edge, copper pipe cut down the center and flattened cuts exceptionally. However, edge retention isn't necessary. For your use, you'll generally take one person out and then ditch it.

If you can make a thin ceramic knife, I urge you to. Depending on your mix, you can have a razor sharp edge that resists breakage and can get through any metal detector.

You cut steel with any stronger steel. The easiest things to get ahold of are toenail clippers or the black paper clips. Nail clippers are stainless, and the black clips are spring steel. Some of the coolest knives I made were from inch and a half wide steel. You can cut it to length, sharpen the hell out of it, wrap you a nice handle, and even make a custom leather case for it. Other pieces consisted of copper pipe that were pounded flat and sharpened on both ends. One of the first was a three-inch long screw from one of the phones that I've ground the threads and head off of, melted between two toothbrushes, and braided a handle on. There used to be long steel clips in the Army duffel bags, after being bent straight, they make a great push dagger. Bathroom tiles are a great source

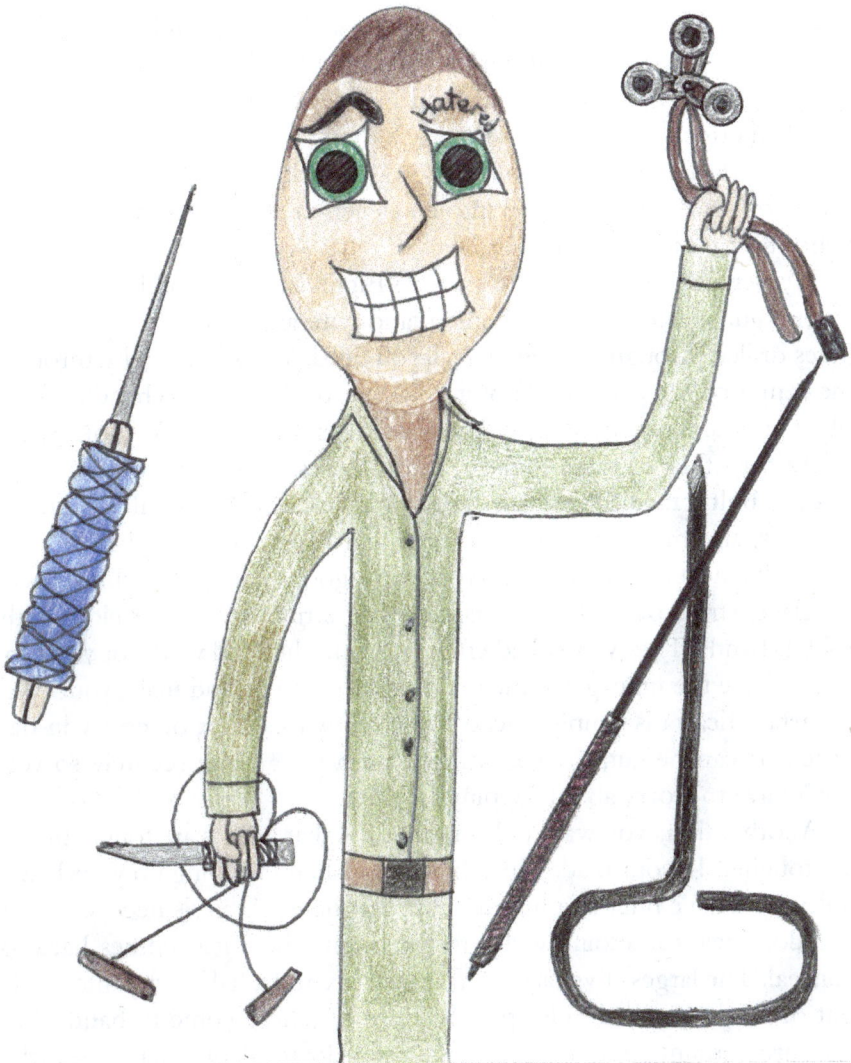

of thin ceramic. All you have to do is score it with a nail clipper and crack along the line. Each 12"x12" tile allows you one thirteen-inch knife and two six-inch knives if you break diagonally. If you break parallel, you can get roughly eight twelve-inch knives.

If you are not able to get your hands on these things easily, try to make a blunt weapon. A blunt trauma weapon is anything heavy and solid enough to inflict damage. One of the easiest I've made was the paper beer can. This consists of soaking sheets of 8.5"x11" paper in the sink and stacking them onto each other. Try fifty to one hundred sheets, more if you're feeling bold. You fold it in half and roll it tightly, you tightly wrap a strip of bed sheet around it and tie it off. This compressed paper wad weighs roughly two pounds and hits very hard. Even after drying, this is an effective weapon.

Another piece I made a while back was a stack of roughly one hundred sheets of soaked paper rolled into an eleven-inch baton. Once wrapped tight, this provides a great club.

My personal favorite is the garrote. Eighteen inches of low E string from a guitar (steel only) or some piano wire and two wood pegs with holes drilled through the center is all you need. You slip the wire through the center of the pegs and knot it up. Now, you've got two handles for a silent, classic weapon. Look online for videos on how to use it properly.

As for other sources, look to light fixtures, fence wire, duffel bags, screws, bolts, medical braces, radio pouches, shelves, bunks, outdoor benches, and maintenance supplies. If you're in need of a handle material, I've never been steered wrong with good old-fashioned bootlace, shoelace, strips of bed sheet, garbage bag string, even light cloth with rubber bands. They've worked effectively and they will work for you too. If you have the time, get some two-part clear epoxy and make your own micarta. Micarta is simply stacked up cloth with a layer of epoxy in between. It can be cut, drilled, and put onto your blade securely so you don't have to worry about slipping.

Another thing you want to be aware of is that bodies are tough, bones are tougher. If your blade hits a bone, your hand is going up your blade unless you have built in a hilt or wrapped one in. A hilt is necessary, but you don't want it adding width to the point where it becomes hard to conceal. The largest I've used so far was a six and a half inch tanto made out of a straightened radio pouch stiffener. These come in handy, but they are certainly not going to pass a pat down. People have used the

composite toes from boots, pencils, melted pens, slivers of toilet seats, and things like that are good for what's known as a "get up off me" where only a bit of damage needs to be inflicted to make a point.

For the most part, simply showing a knife will back down an assailant who is simply attempting to throw their weight around. Once they see that you'll escalate to lethal, they back down. Should you try this on an enemy, you'll be shot dead instantly.

As for blunt weapons, everyone has heard of a lock in a sock or batteries in a sock. Don't try this. After the first couple of hits, the sock rips and your batteries/lock go flying. It's also ineffective if you don't know how to use it. People swing the whole sock which allows the weapon to be easily caught. Should you ever resort to a lock, use two and tie them firmly together, using the sock as a ligature through the loops on the locks. Even then, this will be noisy, but it may be what you need to get attention or make a statement. A set of locks on a tightly tied belt works best but you only allow three to five inches of swing. You can also tightly roll a magazine, loop the belt through the middle and pull a lock into it. This is an improvised hammer. If you've ever seen a Nulla Nulla, this is almost the same thing when used correctly.

One of the biggest failures was the bars of soap and a towel or a sock. The soap crumbles and then you're swinging a misshapen ball of awkward. An easy one was an unopened soda. The bottom of the can is incredibly effective when used against the jaw, nose, throat, and eyes. The back of a hardcover book can also be used effectively when delivering shots to the nose and throat. It will get someone off of you in a hurry. One of the most gruesome used is boiling water mixed thick with magic shave. The only thing worse than that is boiling baby oil or boiling grease. Those will shear the skin off someone instantly and turn them into a lifelong blob of wax, if they survive.

It is noteworthy that silk dental floss can cut steel, but you'll rarely have this in any survival situation under enemy watch. If you're lucky enough to have some, it is a great asset.

Cordage

You'll have to make your own cordage for laces, ties, and whatever else you can think of. All you need is thread. If you're lucky enough to be able to rob a sew shop or harvest thread from socks, pants seams, jumpsuit seams, or elsewhere, you'll need to spin it up. You take into account each strand's tensile strength, what you'll be using it for, and how long you need it to be. You take strands that are twice as long as what you need, tie one end to a bed rail and the other around a pen. You pull this tight and spin it until it begins to bind. You have someone hold the center while you tie the two loose ends together and let it slowly counter spin. You've now made rope. A few spun strands is a great thread saw for plastic and other materials, a few hundred is enough to hold your body weight. You can do this with thread, yarn, strips of bed sheet, or anything that resembles a strand. I've even done this with the metal spiral from a notebook and made my own barbed wire.

Locks

Locks suck, especially when you need to get through one. A lock is nothing more than a tumbler, a case, top pins, bottom pins, and springs to keep tension on the pins. Once the bottom pins are raised to the level of the shear line, the top pins no longer extend into the tumbler and the lock will turn freely. Any higher or lower, and the top pins may still be in the tumbler, or the bottom pins may be pushed out and bind. Check out a set of lock pics online, they often come with clear plastic locks that are fully functional. This will teach you the concept on how to defeat a lock, what each style of pin feels like, and how much tension is necessary for the different types of locks. There are trainers available for combination locks, pad locks, door locks, dead bolts, doorknobs, safes, you name it. It's all available online for under one hundred dollars. All you need, in reality, is a bent piece for a pick and a tension bar to keep tension on the pins. The biggest will click first, then the next biggest, until all the pins have met the shear line. Your lock will pop open.

Not all locks are the same though. Some require inward pressure, some require ridiculous torque, and others have different pin sets on each side. Some of the most secure locks are correctional services locks that have a four-sided key, each side with its own specific cut. It looks like a four-inch long Phillips screwdriver. The lock for this requires hard inward pressure and an immense amount of turning power.

The easiest way to get through a lock is to have the key. If you don't have one, bust open a similar lock. Any lock with a master key is the easiest. You learn the spacing of each pin in the tumbler and the exact height each pin has to be brought to in order to turn the tumbler. By knowing the space and distance, you can make an apparatus that you can slide into the lock and open with a tension bar. Don't even bother with any kind of correctional lock. They're designed well, require odd means to open, and are rotating discs instead of pins. The risk isn't worth the reward.

Picking a lock takes years of experience, breaking one and making a master key takes a day. I won't get into detail on what to do once you break the mechanism out of a lock to access the pins or internal components. This, you'll have to learn on your own. It's much more fun this way and you'll actually learn it correctly.

Where Problems Originate

Most prison breaks fail because of simple mistakes and snitches. Through lawful detention, people can get special treatment from guards for exchange of information, more so when it's vital. During your stay in the enemy's holding facility, you're more likely to be around other dedicated patriots with one thing on their mind, kill the enemy and get out of there. Snitching can still be a problem since there will be middle-people stuck there for no reason, left wingers confused as right and vice versa, and even people working for the other side. Once you get established, get a feel for who everyone is. The only people that should know anything about the plan, or that there is even a plan, are your strategic assets. Close neighbors that you have a good history with, those with weapons and tools, those with combat experience, former law enforcement, trusted people who have a nearby hideout, trusted people with a nearby vehicle or means of extraction, and medical personnel. Once you get out, it's back to evasion mode only you're being hunted.

Those key people will know how to move around the area, where safe houses are, and have people who can provide help. The former law enforcement will help greatly in avoiding search patterns and the medical personnel will be able to treat whatever injuries happen during the operation or during the extraction.

Planning

First, you never plan, you prepare. You know decently where the enemy will be holding prisoners and have cache locations nearby. Know where these are at in reference to direction and leave subtle markers to assist you on an extraction. The first major part of getting out is to plan it before you get in. Your cache will not only need your supplies but supplies for the others that made the break possible. I'd advise several firearms, plenty of high protein food, inclement weather clothing, and a few tarps for shelter. Just remember, you'll be hunted once they discover that you're gone.

This is where bushcraft comes in handy. You may need to eat off the land, live in the earth, evade enemy air assets, and know how to follow each other. Get ahold of the Army Survival Manual and a few other books written by Green Berets on bushcraft. I'm so vague when it comes to books because I want you to buy the wrong ones. I want you to go through five or ten books and learn from all of them. I want you to study diligently and by giving you a simple book title, you won't read beyond that. Your survival depends on your ability to study, retain information, and that you can apply what you've learned. This is the reason why I tell you consistently to go out into the woods and practice each skill until you're good at it then begin teaching others.

These simple tricks give you a signature based on how you do each one and these are signatures that only your loved ones will remember.

I would get into the how-to methods of getting out but they're irrelevant. Any plan that I could give you can quickly be ruined by enemy actions. You will have to study their actions in the now, react to them, know their vulnerabilities, know how each member of your team is feeling at that time, and execute your plan when the opportunity presents itself. No one, no matter how much they tell you, has a fool-proof plan. You could consult an expert who is deep underground at Florence ADMAX, and they can give you all sorts of plans, however, if your team is sick, hurt, or otherwise in a bind, the plan goes out the window. Situations evolve instantly. An enemy action that only took a minute can foil the whole thing and you must be able to react to this.

Once you decide to execute the plan, there's no going back. Hesitation will get you caught or killed. When you're actually over their lines, the follow-through is the determinant of whether or not the plan worked.

You'll need to move extremely far, incredibly fast. This is where strategically placed cache sites come in and you'll use your bushcraft to hide your trail. Dogs are a menace but there are things you can do. Nothing will hide your scent from a trained dog but even the most trained dog has to be able to walk or at least have a nose to track you. That's all I'll say about that.

During your plan, it pays to sabotage as much of the enemy's equipment as possible. If you can disable several vehicles, sever communication lines, screw their barracks doors shut, or even burn them alive inside, you'll be glad you did. Set traps, disable their ability to follow you, kill their morale and make them want to quit following, and go on the offense. Just don't jeopardize the mission to do these things. If needed, you can leave a squirter or two behind that will wait until you're gone then begin these things. They strategically wait until you're gone and then begin the sabotage phase, ending it with burning the barracks and command post. Then they exit through the same means that you did but run in a different direction.

This chapter was short due to the fact that I wrote it in federal prison. Due to the operational security, it's not smart to advertise knowledge in certain fields and this is one of those fields. It's also noteworthy that although I disagree with my conviction, my confinement is lawful so I'm not a major pain in their ass. I don't study them because I don't give a shit what they do, and they also feign disorganized to disrupt monitoring operations. These folks are Americans just like me and are doing a job that they are under oath to complete. Their motivation is to keep the rapists and murderers off our streets. Though many of us dispute the legality of our confinement, it's the system as a whole that must change. The staff are simply cogs who are supporting their families.

Now, we get into what to do when you're out.

Chapter 7

—⟡—

Bring The Fight To Them

S o, you've managed to survive the torture, interrogations, the inhospitable treatment by the enemy, and get yourself out of there, in the sense that you've exited the building and are executing a plan. Believe it or not, this phase begins before the last. Everything you did could be better.

Assuring Your Survival Begins Now

Once you initiate your plan, the sabotage phase immediately begins and never truly ends. If you want to stay free from enemy captivity, you'll have to use every advantage that you have available.

Through your time studying the enemy, you know when they conduct weapons maintenance, where their motor pool is at, where their armory is at, where their ammo point is at, where each posted guard is at, their personnel rotation, shift change, how quickly they can reinforce, and their response time to emergencies. Their diligence in conducting their operations is a direct reflection of how diligently they will hunt you down. Listen diligently for counter signs, set up observation on keypads to watch number sequences, and look where doors are activated from. Listen for their call signs and how they call on the radio. "Hey you, this is me" versus "this is me, hey you."

To put major wrenches in their abilities, you need to hit several key places while your exit team prepares the route. Should you be executing your plan during the dumbass shift, the opportunity arises to screw doors closed, sabotage every vehicle, break things off in each one of their key holes, cut their communication and electrical lines, and set traps all over the place to mess with them further.

Should you be able to hit their armory, it's likely guarded and secured by a solid means. If this is the case, set a large fire outside of it so that those responding to your plan will not be able to get the door open. Remember, their reinforcements are only effective if they have the means to fight you. If you find the armory to be a simple secured room, gain access and take out the armorer. Grab whatever weapons you can and then hit the ammo point. It's vital that you burn whatever is left. Before exiting the armory, burn it to disable all weapons that you're leaving behind. Before leaving the ammo point, start a large fire which will surely lead to a massive explosion and fireworks show. This will greatly impact their abilities to begin searching for you and limit their available resources. Very few enemies will want to hunt an armed person while they are unarmed. Gain control of the command post/control center in order to cut their communications, camera feed, and whatever else you can find in it. If you can't control it, cut every wire leading into it and burn it.

Should the enemy have a personal vehicle lot, get their plate numbers before you leave entirely. License plate numbers will lead you straight to the owner's address and allow you to take them out at your leisure. After you have the plate numbers, slash their tires so that they can't use their personal vehicles in a pursuit.

The Possible Outcomes

Let's say you got lucky, the dumbest individuals and the lazy were on shift. You've assembled a perfect crew, taken out every guard on shift, you control the command post/control center, the armory and ammo, the motor pool, and everything else. Keep their facility to yourself and make sure that everyone is armed, your own guards are posted, and try to elicit information out of the guards you decided to keep. Know where the other facilities are at, what their guard roster looks like, and whether or not the facilities are in regular communication. The current facility allows you to maintain a safe base of operations and organize your next move.

If their **dumbass shift** wasn't on, you'll be at a disadvantage but can still get out. If you didn't get so lucky, don't worry. Through diligent sabotage operations, you can cripple their means to follow you. You can use their **asshole shift** to make them overreact and allow you to gain access to the same points. While they're busy chasing down a single runner, you can send a few to each of the key points and conduct unrestricted sabotage operations while they're distracted. Perhaps you can fake them out into believing that you succeeded. You can then wait until they send out search parties, assuring that they have left a bare minimum crew behind. You can take out what's left and simply fight off the others when they return. Either way you choose, the object is still to get out. After that, run far and fast.

No matter who is on, your outcomes should be in the middle of these two extremes. Use the chaos and frenzy to monopolize at every opportunity.

In The Clear

Your first task after getting out of the fence is to get to a cache site. You need to change clothes, arm yourself properly, eat, and make a tentative plan of your next move. The hardasses will want to track you down to be seen as the higher skilled but they may be cowards, hoping to never actually cross paths with you. When it becomes a matter of life and death, many men are simply not prepared to face this. Other guards will be concerned for their safety as it is and will be thinking, "I just work here to make ends meet." These people will be of almost no consequence to you, even if they happen to notice anomalies that would lead them to you. The dumbasses and lazy crew will usually quit their jobs or avoid the assignment entirely. Once you get farther than they are willing to follow, you're good to go and are able to get things professionally established.

This is the phase when you become the most effected by getting to a bug out location, compile everyone's knowledge, and assign tasks. It is vital after this that everyone splits up and you no longer use this bug out site. People know where it is now and may tell the enemy later. You are now on the offense and each person acting should be a lone wolf. The information on their positions, defenses, weak spots, prisoner holding areas, and the rest of the facility is known by all. Each is to use this knowledge accordingly and conduct operations at will.

Psychological Warfare

Psychological warfare defeats more enemies than bullets and bombs combined. If you make the enemy lose all morale, reason to fight, and begin questioning their own leaders, you've effectively won the war. One severely mutilated partner is all it takes to make reality sink in. They begin to see that they are vulnerable. Your main job is to strike fear into every enemy that is still alive, remind them of their dead partners, hit them at home, and give them no peace. No one can defend everywhere, all the time. You monopolize on these vulnerabilities to torment the enemy in such a way that Marquis de Sade would try to talk sense into you. You begin this cycle of fear production by doing a few things each day, none of which are incredibly hard. It's the creepy reminders of what you're capable of that keep the enemy on their toes. The fear of pain is more effective than the pain itself.

Sabotage

Once vehicles become candles, claymores begin spraying their route home, photos of their family show up on their windshield, their partners are slain in the parking lot, men are lit ablaze at work, bodies are hung on display in public, horrific dissections are conducted on bodies strategically placed, and little friendly notes are placed on their home, they begin to freak out. They report the incident which spreads the news like wildfire, especially when it happens to several people they know. Alerts go out, pictures circulate, and rumors expand, the next thing you know, you've got credit for things that you've never done. The mark of your group is feared more than death itself. You begin this hell cycle by locating them.

By getting their plate numbers, you now have their names and addresses. Vital records databases, public information, voter registration, genealogy sites, and information brokers have all of their information. Addresses, phone numbers, relatives, members of their households, political affiliation, criminal history, and whatever else you want to know. Since you have acquaintances who did not make it out of the camp, it's time to get rid of more enemies, the slick way. You track down their house and spray paint "found you" across the front, leave notes on their car saying, "find a new line of work," or begin operations on their home. You can sit in the distance and take pictures of their family as they enter and exit the home. You send a photo to the enemy saying, "Is this worth it to keep your job?" Many will find a new line of work.

Should you have killed some of the enemies in your operation, leave notes for the others saying, "you're next." Many of the less dedicated enemies will find a way out of their job.

Simply leaving a note on their door that says, "you shall pay for your spouse's sins," is enough to upend someone's family life. Once the family no longer feels safe at home, they'll surely leave, or they'll prepare for a fight. Either of which gives them no peace.

Since you know their shifts, you can rig devices to their vehicles or lie in wait with the distance rifle. Once these things start happening, they'll realize that their command, their numbers, and their peers cannot keep them safe. This will severely breakdown their morale and leave them questioning their government's agenda. Things like this will purge all who are not absolutely dedicated to the cause.

Light their cars on fire, hurl Molotov cocktails into their buildings and at their homes, rig OC to tripwires or pressure plates, rig up napalm sprayers out of lawn sprinklers, use ghost riding fuel trucks to wreak havoc against them. Do simple things like set smoke bombs, whistling fireworks, or laughing dolls on their routes, anything to put pressure on them and see that they could already be dead. Leave notes saying, "there won't be a second chance." This lets them know that you've just reached them and even their armed partners could not stop it.

Many of the enemy are there simply because of orders that post them there. Even the hardasses will begin to rethink things once a picture of their family is left under their windshield wiper.

If you succeed in these operations, the enemy will be run thin on personnel and there will be major security breaches at the camp. This allows you to conduct a better rescue operation to free the others.

If you ever get a chance to shoot one, make it a headshot. You want to be able to keep their uniforms. By taking accurate shots during a shift change, a team in a pickup truck can cruise through, collecting bodies and weapons. These items can have infinite uses, especially if you seize a camp and pose as the enemy.

When you conduct rescue operations, interview each person separately. They'll tell you who the sympathizers and rats are. Execute them. See who has been thoroughly vetted and is willing to help your operation. Brief these individuals as you did back at the bug out shack and have them conduct lone wolf operations. Occasionally, form small teams and take on big objectives. Take an armory, take an ammo point, take a motor pool, take a camp, and whatever else is vulnerable. The more people you can use for operations, the better, as long as they're trained in operation security postures. The last thing you want is to find out that they're posting videos of what you do or use their phones during operations. GPS is everywhere and it can have deadly consequences. You have to be extremely careful with who you trust, especially when the government will pay large amounts of money for your information.

Perhaps snitching on your bug out location will earn someone $50,000. Your name may be worth $10,000. Your family's names may be worth $5,000 each. Your base of operations could yield $100,000. There may even be a price on your head for $3 million. At that point, it doesn't even matter if the enemy has money, there will be contract takers that you'd never expect.

Your imagination, assets, situation, and motivation are your only limits when it comes to bringing the fight to their doorstep. The more equipment you have, the more options you have to hit them with. If a conventional force is deployed against you, you have opportunities to seize their vehicles, uniforms, body armor, heavy and light machine guns, grenades and grenade launchers, breach charges and high explosives, det cord, shock tube, and more ammunition than you'll know what to do with.

You can do the noble thing and dedicate your life to freeing the wrongly captured or you can choose to disappear completely. As long as you make it out of the enemy's territory, you can link up with friendly troops abroad and earn an honest living amongst them. You can become the average citizen again and live a normal life or continue to train like a true war fighter. You can simply refit everything you need, get a crew of iron patriots together with some armored vehicles, and wage actual war against the enemy. Whatever you choose to do, that's up to you. Just be mindful that there are others still in captivity, others suffering horribly at the hands of the enemy, and it will continue until each of them are dead or too scared to continue operations. Those who backed down, will later resurface as competent enemies if they still believe in the cause.

Remember when we left Iraq? ISIS came to power. Remember when we left Afghanistan? The Taliban took over. Once you leave the battle-field, whatever you didn't kill will quickly come after you. You have to realize that they are forever a new person because of what they went through by your hands. The lost friends, the lost memories, perhaps severe injuries are now crippling them. Once you kill one, you might as well handle them all.

Whether or not you believe this, whether or not it applies to your needs, it's a reality that is lived around the world. A reality that has gone on for thousands of years. Tribal warfare dominates lands over small issues far in the distant past. Look at the Hatfields and McCoys, look at the Afghan tribes, look at the religious strife that's been wild for millennia. Unless people give up extremist beliefs, the only way they will ever stop is death. Even then, they believe that their death is noble, killing you is virtuous, and extinguishing your bloodline is the path to whatever goal they have.

Chapter 8

The More You Know . . .

I was told years ago to become the evil that the victims wish existed, to be the evil that most Americans pretend doesn't exist, the black hearted monster that can do whatever is necessary to ensure the safety of their people. I'm a firm believer that there are no good nor bad actions, only actions. The way that you choose to apply them is what determines whether it is good or bad. Killing is wrong but when done to protect your life or your family, it becomes good. If you kill for your nation, no one bats an eye. Stealing is wrong but stealing to protect lives is justified easily. If you steal nuclear launch codes from the enemy, no one bats an eye. Lying is wrong but lying to trick an enemy is justified. If there's a group of people killing members of your group and you deny affiliation, no one bats an eye. These scenarios can be applied to almost any position in life. If you think you are not a liar, have you taught your kids about Santa or the Easter Bunny? Have you told them that their favorite pet ran away to a farm after it was hit by a car? If you can justify these things, you can justify doing whatever is necessary to preserve your life and the lives of those you love. If you're willing to lie to those you love, you'll be able to kill someone who is threatening you.

In a war, the only way to stop atrocities, rape of your people, and secure your God-given rights is to kill anyone who threatens it. Make no mistake, war is absolute hell, innocents get killed in the middle of it, and rape happens no matter who is in charge. Think our people wouldn't? Look at how many World War II veterans were hanged for rape of the locals. Look at how many Vietnam veterans are in prison over the rape and murder of innocents. Look at how many War on Terror veterans are in prison for rape and murder. We are all human; we all have that inner dark side which is willing to destroy others for our personal gain. During war, people go through changes that not even they understand. The adrenaline, the rage, the hatred. What one man has done, so are we just as capable.

Will you be the man who sits by and watches this happen, or will you be the one who gets up and fights righteously on the field of battle? Anyone who is not the latter does not deserve the rights that they exercise. They have no place in a society that they would watch crippled by an enemy. To repel these sorts of enemies, which is anyone wishing to conquer you, you must employ every skill and tool available to you, inflict heinous atrocities against their warriors, and guard your people closely.

The first seven chapters of this book laid the groundwork, the basic ideas and skills to build off of. What you do with this information, how you continue to grow it, is entirely up to you. If things really do go awry, you'll be lucky to make it out alive with what you've learned here. You'll be beaten, broken, scarred mentally, and forever changed. In addition to this, you'll have to brave the elements, animals, rebel groups who wish to rob you, the enemy, and the prison of your own mind. Being "switched on" constantly has devastating consequences if you are not prepared to deal with them.

The only way to lessen this pain is to expand your knowledge base now. Be prepared to see and endure what the enemy will do to you and your family, learn every skill that you can now, and become adept at survival. Every little thing that you can learn now is one more thing that you can apply when everything collapses. You should never stop building your Bookshelf, you should study at every opportunity, and you should continue to build a competent group. See how I keep repeating these things? It is because it matters more than anything else.

The more trustworthy people you have in your group, the more knowledge you have at your disposal. You can team up with others who have knowledge that accents yours. Team up with skilled professionals who can provide expertise to your operations. Doctors, architects, engineers, special forces veterans, and others that are at the top of their field will play major roles in your community. With these people, you do not require as much knowledge since you have others there who are adept. These people can teach their skills to all and make the collective whole stronger.

You should never be afraid to apply your sense of humor to this stuff. Human nature is to try to predict what will happen in the future, let your mind run wild across all options. You may find a scenario that your enemy has thought of and then be ready for it. By imagining outlandish things, you'll then be prepared and slightly disappointed at hard struggles since they were not interesting enough. This helps you keep a calm, cool, and collected thought process through your tasks. Remember, the hardass is blinded by his only view. Don't be like him. Keep an open mind and never discourage any input, no matter how ridiculous it sounds.

While in Helmand, we went over every possible outcome, to include the Taliban mobilizing a tank. We sit, we go over all sorts of possibilities, and we prepare for the worst. It's good to remember that desperate men will do desperate things. Once someone's back is against the wall, they will act out in fear. They make serious mistakes, cause irreparable harm, and usually end up severely injured.

Now, I'm going to stress this again, you can never have too many bug out locations. No matter how small, your location is a lifesaving shelter with supplies. Even if it's only a week worth of supplies, it's far more than you have if you had to leave empty handed to save your life. A good meal, a change of clothes, a weapon, and a good night's rest may be all you need to rise up and fight successfully.

I've discussed communication a lot. Have you thought into how your group will communicate? Morse code and sign language come in handy more than you think. If you can't make noise due to operational security, sign language is priceless. If you can't see each other or hear words, tapping out phrases in Morse may be your only option. Morse code can be done using taps, scratches, light flashes, blows of a horn, or any means that allows "dits" and "dahs." I fully recommend learning the alphabets for Greek, Russian, Arabic, and runes. Even if you don't speak the language, you can spell things out phonetically. These can also be used in all sorts of codes.

Hand signals are another major asset. Know your own military's and the enemy's hand signals. Beyond this is practicing different handwriting styles. If your enemy uses a handwriting database, they'll know who has written what by logging exemplars. For instance, the United States uses the Forensic Information System of Handwriting, known as FISH. Sometimes it pays to be anonymous. Sending questionable messages in your handwriting can be detrimental.

Imagine that every piece of information you retain is another bullet in the magazine. Life is but a gunfight and it pays to have plenty of ammo. I'm hoping that this book sparks your creativity, that you take what I've planted the seed for and make it grow. You need to combine all this with a fully stocked Bookshelf that educates you in every facet of a secure lifestyle. Knowledge will one day save your life, I guarantee it. Knowledge has been an indispensable asset throughout my wild teenage years, my time in the Army, my life in general adulthood, and absolutely key to my survival in federal prison.

If you can't look yourself in the mirror and honestly tell yourself "I can survive in a war, I can survive in prison, I can prosper through any struggle," you're not trained or educated enough. You need continuous learning. If you're one of the few people who can, quit kidding your-self and learn some more. Confidence can be a killer, this is why highly trained men continue to make life altering mistakes. It's your job to be humble, learn from those who know far more than you do, and always push forward.

What you don't continually practice and use, you will lose. Most skills are perishable, even though others are stuck with us for the rest of our lives. Honestly, I can tell you the serial number of my M-4, ACOG, PEQ-15, Nods, MBITR, Rifleman radio, and the EUD that I carried on my first deployment, but I can't for the life of me remember how many pounds of torque is proper on an AR barrel nut. This is why it's import-ant to practice, train, and seek education as if your life depended on it, because it does. Not only your life, but the lives of your friends, family, and even strangers that you form an alliance with.

Get Dedicated

Take time and go extreme camping, go up in the snow deserts and camp, camp in the sand dunes, camp in the swamp, camp in a pine thick-et, just make sure that the first time you have to do this is not because you're in danger and forced to. Know your gear inside and out, know what works and what doesn't, know your limits and how to get stronger.

If you're really dedicated to the cause, enlist in the Army with an in-fantry contract, carry it further to an Option 40 or 18X contract. If you have community ties, go through the police academy or look into Federal law enforcement. Their credentials alone will be all you need to stay out of the storm, even when you're in the wrong.

Or At Least Get Serious

If you're not looking for a balls-to-the-wall job like that, consider the National Guard, the Army Reserves, or the Sheriff's Department reserve. There are survival courses available at all levels across the nation, tactical ranges which will teach you how to operate, three gun competitions, ob-stacle runs, and all sorts of opportunities to test yourself. Wherever you live, there's probably one near you. If you look online, you'll see people from all walks of life participating in these events on a regular basis. Before I got locked up, there was a 12-year-old girl that was sponsored in three gun competitions. If she can do it, you can do it. All it takes is effort, practice, and time. There are whole families out there that practice several martial arts to stay safe in urban environments. Several communities hold regular events simply to train first aid and emergency response.

Why Wait?

Each and every day is another opportunity to get stronger, get faster, lift more, grow your mind, strengthen family bonds, train your friends, and prepare. Every single step you take today is one less step you'll have to take tomorrow. Will you be the guy at the finish line wishing he'd already run faster, knowing that he could have pushed harder? This situation in real life translates out to you and your family starving, out of ammunition in a gunfight, wishing you'd done more today.

Your time to act is now, your time to train is now, and your life is still in your hands. You should already be in full kit with a ruck on your back, suppressor on, and headed for the starting line of the 12 mile. Your enemy is training to kill you right now and has been doing it while smoking whiskey flavored cigars, so why aren't you getting serious yet?

Chapter 9

Eat Right

Nutrition is a force multiplier. If you're in a calorie deficit, you're going to be miserable. If you're surviving off of packaged snack cakes, your head is going to be killing you, you'll lose muscle, and you'll be miserable. Sometimes, it pays to go for the right stuff. Look into natural nutrition and get a few books on how to maintain your body in peak physical condition. Get yourself some good advice from a nutritionist, look into super foods and how to prepare them, and look into eating naturally.

It is also important to go into these situations knowing that you may meet up with others that will also need to eat. Whether it's family, friends, or others you want to add to your group, make sure that you have enough food for everyone before you join up. The last thing you want to do is be left without supplies. Should you decide to enter into an agreement, make sure that the terms are laid out clearly, just as you would with an important contract.

Here's an example of a one year pantry, at a minimum.

One Year Pantry

500 pounds of whole grain wheat
200 pounds of flour
100 pounds of cornmeal
200 pounds of oats
50 pounds of quinoa
300 pounds of rice
200 pounds of pasta
150 pounds of dried refried beans
50 pounds of lentils
40 pounds of split peas
80 pounds of **good** peanut butter
10 gallons of dehydrated eggs
50 pounds of TVP whatever the hell that is (I still have no idea, but I'm told by a health nut in here to keep it)
50 pounds of Millet (also have no idea what this is)
400 pounds of sugar
50 pounds of real local honey
40 pounds of Maple syrup
40 pounds of jam

40 gallons of vegetable oil
300 pounds of dry milk
20 pounds of baking powder
20 pounds of baking soda
20 pounds of yeast
100 pounds of salt
10 gallons of vinegar
50 pounds of chicken bouillon
50 pounds of beef bouillon
100 packs of tuna
100 packs of canned meat
40 pounds of home dried jerky
About 50 summer sausages
100 gallons of jarred marinara
50 gallons of jarred Alfredo
10 gallons of your favorite dehydrated fruits (each)
10 gallons of your favorite dehydrated vegetables (each)
10 pounds of butter powder
200 pounds of Mass Gainer (to get jacked)
Your regular daily vitamins and supplements (your daily use times 365)
A few of each of your favorite assorted condiments
1200 pounds of charcoal
5 cords of firewood
10 gallons of gasoline and oil
12 fluoride toothpaste with toothbrushes (to make sure you have teeth to enjoy it all)

Some Super Foods

Arugula and Water grass combined, purslane, chickweed, Green lettuce and cabbage combined, broccoli with cauliflower and Brussels sprouts combined, carrots and tomatoes combined, onions and garlic combined, kale, collard/mustard greens, okra, mushrooms, pomegranates, all edible berries, elderberry, flax seeds, sunflower seeds, chia seeds, oregano, Echinacea, local honey, cinnamon, and guava are said to be some of the best. Oregano is an antibiotic and cinnamon is a natural pain reliever. Pine needle tea is packed with vitamin C.

Anti-Angiogenics

Onions, tomatoes, turmeric, Macha, all edible berries, black rice, cinnamon, citrus fruits, cruciferous vegetables, seeds, ginger, grapes, green tea, Omega threes, Peppers, quince, resveratrol, soybeans (careful, these produce estrogen), and spinach.

Fine, I confess, that's more than a years' worth of supplies but I prefer to eat happily. I also didn't include water use. This is a touchy subject with many conflicting opinions so I'm leaving you to do your own work and planning for it. Personally, I'd find a way to get a hundred-thousand-gallon water tank with a well and rain collection system. I prefer showers. As for the food listed, I prefer good, balanced meals that will actually do the job I expect them to. I figure that if I'm going to go through the trouble of the stocking, preparations, and cooking, I'm going to enjoy each and every meal. In the world, when I was regularly doing twelve-mile rucks, lots of PT, and my own shenanigans, I had a high-in-everything diet. Every meal seemed to be either spaghetti or Alfredo (with plenty of beef or chicken), sided with macaroni and cheese and mashed potatoes, cheese stuffed croissants, and a generous helping of alcohol. The days off were large stuffed crust pizzas, huge lasagnas, pork chops with the same sides, steaks with the same sides, or we tear up a restaurant. Coming back from a field rotation, we always went out. I know what you're thinking, macaroni and cheese, mashed potatoes, and cheese stuffed croissants? Well, if you're not happy, life quickly goes to shit, and these are wonderful foods. I enjoyed the health issues that go along with it all.

If you've got the time and resources, I recommend having large caches of supply like this all over the place. For instance, if I'm maintaining a base of operations in northern Michigan, I'd plan to have one of these cache warehouses as Far East as Sault St. Marie, L'Anse, Marquette, and Wakefield. I would expand into Wisconsin to places like Hurley, Ashland, Superior, Mercer, and at locations across the vast expanse of farmland. From there, I'd expand to Minnesota, Illinois, Iowa, and Missouri. If you space your supplies out far and can keep them hidden, you've got years of food stored. Should nature strike, you may lose one site, but you'll have plenty more. At each location, you can live comfortably for a year or more before having to leave. The one-hundred mile treks will take a couple of weeks if you're moving comfortably and camping. This is far enough to get you out of any bad situations. You may even consider leaving an area that's taken over by less than cordial enemy. If you can't fight them, leave and plot to kill them later.

I further recommend that you look deeply into Superfoods, resveratrol, natural medicinal teas, natural allergy remedies, anti-carcinogens, adaptogens, nerves, restorative tonics, and Nootropic herbs. The "health nuts" in here tell me to look into this stuff but can't explain what any of it is. They simply read this in nutrition books and give the advice so I'm doing the same. Do your research into all of this and find which good diet works for you. Find which super foods you want to be ground finely and add it to your mass gainer or health shakes.

With all of the assets out there at your disposal, it really doesn't pay to put more than this into the chapter. You've been given a good pantry list and the right ideas for your own research. Should you have family with medicinal conditions, look up the foods that ease their symptoms. There are natural pain remedies out there that work well. Cinnamon is one of them.

Disclaimer

"These statements have not been evaluated by the United States Food and Drug Administration, they are not intended to treat, diagnose, prevent, or cure any disease." These recommendations are based off of the experiences of several people who have had great effects from a healthy diet, and I strongly urge you to speak with your doctor and a nutritionist before developing any plans for exercise or diet.

For the next chapter of this book, I'm shifting gears to break up the style a bit. Just as I've done with a disclaimer, it's important to know the laws and what you are within your rights to do.

Chapter 10

What You Need To Know

I'm sure you've heard it many times throughout your life, "Ignorance of the law excuses no one." Let's break this down. Lawyers have to go through a four-year school just to get into a three-year law school. They must complete law school to sit for the Bar exam. They have to pass the Bar exam before they can legally practice law. Yet, the average citizen, with none of that, can be held criminally or civilly liable for breaking any of the laws. When you compile state civil and criminal laws, The United States Code, and the court's rules, this mound of paper is going to weigh hundreds of pounds.

I don't personally know anyone who has ever read such a large book and I am willing to bet that you haven't either. Yet, if you break anyone of the thousands of laws, you're going to be held liable. To fully understand the law though, you need a Juris Doctorate and have passed the Bar, in the eyes of the law. The deck is clearly stacked against you.

When I mixed up my slurry out in the woods, where I believed to be alone, there wasn't any inkling of worry within me that thought I was violating the International Chemical Weapons Convention. As a reasonable and prudent person, I was playing around out in the woods, far from anyone. Yet, all it took was an investigation and the phrase "Ignorance of the law is no excuse." I'm now sitting in Federal Prison on a 135 month sentence for a law I never knew existed.

The main problem I had was not knowing where in the law to look. I didn't know there were Civil and Criminal laws. I didn't know there were Rules of Civil Procedure and Rules of Criminal Procedure, let alone Local Rules of each for each court. I didn't know there were Rules of Evidence. I certainly didn't know that these existed at the State and Federal level. The research and study of law is a complex task that requires a lot of time and effort. I fully recommend that you take a paralegal course to familiarize yourself with all of this to prepare for the event that the government claims that you broke a law. You may have a defense written in the law that you wouldn't otherwise see, and be time barred for not raising a valid defense soon enough. It's a giant maze of shenanigans.

So, we're going to cover some of the laws that are tempting to break. For various reasons, survivalists can inadvertently break these laws without knowing it and still be held liable. Keep in mind, I am not a licensed attorney. As a paralegal, I simply prepare documents and do research. Here is a product of the research that I've done. To avoid any copyright problems, I haven't stated in the restatements as they are the property of the program that I use. By looking at the code and the title, you can easily find these laws in the United States Code which is readily available on the Internet.

Here's An Example of How To Read A Federal Law:

Title	Source	Section
18	United States Code (USC)	2332
22	Code of Federal Regulations (CFR)	121.1

As you can see, that's Title 18 of the USC Section 2332. The second is Title 22 CFR Section 121.1.

Now, here's some more titles and what each generally correspond to:

Title 18 Criminal Section
18 USC 16 Defines a Crime of Violence
18 USC Chapter 7 Assault (there are several sections in this chapter).
18 USC 112 Extends protection to Foreign officials, official guests, and internationally protected persons.
18 USC 115 Influencing, Impeding, or Retaliating against a Federal official.
18 USC 175 Biological Weapons
18 USC 229 Chemical Weapons (what I got convicted of)
18 USC 231 Civil disorders (riots).
18 USC 232 Definitions associated with section 231.
18 USC 249 Hate Crimes.
18 USC 401 Power of the Court (contempt section)
18 USC 521 Criminal Street Gangs
18 USC 842 Prohibited Acts involving explosives
18 USC 842(p) distribution of information regarding explosives, destructive devices and weapons of mass destruction.
18 USC 921 Definitions of weapons and prohibited items.
18 USC 922 Unlawful Acts- prohibits certain people from possessing firearms (felons in possession).
18 USC 923 Licenses.
18 USC 924 Penalties.
18 USC 925 Exemptions (felons can possess firearms in certain situations).

Crooked prosecutors stand on the Scales of Justice.

18 USC 929 Use of Restricted Ammunition (AP, incendiary, etc.).
18 USC 1001 False Statements Under Oath, False Declarations.
18 USC 1111 Murder.
18 USC 1112 Manslaughter.
18 USC 1113 Attempted Murder or Manslaughter.
18 USC 1114 Protection of Officers and Government Employees.
18 USC 1512 Tampering with a Witness, Victim, or Informant.
18 USC 1513 Retaliating against a Witness, Victim, or Informant.
18 USC 1515 Definitions Related to Sections 1512 and 1513.
18 USC 2241 War Crimes.
18 USC 2242 Recruitment of Child Soldiers.
18 USC 2283 Transportation of Chemical, Biological, Radiological, Nuclear Weapons or Explosives.
18 USC 2332 Weapons of Mass Destruction.
18 USC 2339 Receiving Training from a Foreign Terrorist Group.
18 USC Chapter 115 Treason, Sedition, and Subversive Acts, (there are many sections to this).
18 USC 2390 Enlistment to Serve Against the United States

Title 21 Controlled Substances/Drugs

21 USC 802 Controlled Substance List (a comprehensive list of every controlled substance or illegal drug).

Title 22

22 USC Chapter 75 Chemical Weapons Convention Implementation Act
22 USC 6701 Definitions and Formulas of Listed Chemical Weapons

Title 26 Taxes

26 USC 5845 Definitions of Taxable items (short barrel rifles or shotguns, Fully automatic weapons, Any Other Weapon, Explosives and Destructive devices)
26 USC 5861 Prohibited Acts (why items listed in 5845 are illegal without taxation)
26 USC 7206 Fraud and False Statements on Taxes

The actual **United States Code** is comprised of **50 Titles** which are **Volumes of Law**. Each Title comprises a large book, all fifty of them require a shelf of epic proportion.

Federal Regulations

When we get into the code of Federal Regulations (CFR) it is also a large compilation of volumes. The CFR publishes the federal policies of every agency in its control. Each agency then develops local policies that may add a more stringent standard than what the CFR requires.

The CFR is a great source of information on how each Federal agency, from OSHA all the way to the FBI and CIA, manage their affairs. Regulations on chemical safety, highway transportation, reporting criteria, food service safety, and anything you can think of are compiled in the CFR.

A section to look into is the United States Munitions List which is 22 CFR 121. Simply looking up the USML online will bring you to an in-depth list of every weaponized substance, weapon, countermeasure, and piece of equipment in the United States Arsenal. Another key place to look is 15 CFR 710. Should you mess with any item listed, you should consult a lawyer on whether or not you're safe in doing so. If you don't consult a lawyer, you'll quickly need a priest once you see what the government will do to you.

WHOA!

Just because you are following the law in accordance with the USC, you may be held liable for Serious fines or penalties for breaking the guidelines set forth in the CFR. Your main regulations are in the CFR and can have severe civil penalties for their violation. There's the Law and then there's the Regulation. Whichever you break, you will be held accountable for.

To put each into perspective, several Titles of the USC have sections that number into the 5 or even 6 digits, meaning that the Title has over ten thousand sections, each with its own respective definitions. Several sections in the CFR are as long or even longer. For instance, 22 CFR part 121 has 121.1, 121.2, etc. and can have all the way up to double or triple decimal digits before getting to part 122. The numbers can be ridiculously long. On the computer, I had to scroll several hundred pages between sections. While scrolling the USC, each section will be followed by supporting case law. Some of these have up to five thousand, yes, 5000 sections of case law after the several page law. The constitution itself is several hundred-thousand pages long because of this exact reason. The supporting case law is organized by circumstance and each circumstance may have several hundred pages of case law. The Fifth Amendment has over 100 pages of **circumstance links** and each **link** may have hundreds of cases attached to it.

Well, how does it feel to be the average citizen having to do the same research as a Juris Doctorate just to avoid insane fines or prison time? It's all possible to sort through but there's never enough time to do thorough enough research.

The law doesn't care that you haven't learned the law in school, that you wouldn't know what to do with it because of the way it's organized or haven't taken the decade to learn it. If you mess up, you're being held accountable.

Look at all the cases for Ineffective Assistance of Counsel and Prosecutorial Misconduct. Look into all the Habeas Corpus filings. These are severe mistakes made by experienced lawyers because they "simply didn't know the law" which entitled prisoners to relief. Hundreds of these issues are litigated in courts across America daily. Experienced lawyers have demonstrated that they **don't know the law**, but you as a private citizen will be held accountable when you break one.

It's time to do some diligent research or at least browse through the Titles of each so you know where to find things if you ever need to. There are several programs out there available for purchase that are used by law firms across the nation. Some can be expensive and are a by-the-minute charge to use but they are up to date, easy to use, and they're reliable.

Chapter 11

Guidance

Our reality is not PTSD. Our reactions to seemingly "normal" stimuli are muscle memory reactions from years of intense training. We may react unfavorably in certain situations, but this is simply because we have seen life in a different light. We cannot unsee what we have been through, it's a permanent part of us.

I've been programmed by some of the best war fighters on earth. Programmed for a combative reality which many of us dabble in frequently. Without our programmed reactions, we would be dead on the battlefield. It's not something we can simply switch off when it becomes an inconvenience to you.

The threats are there, in our homeland. Terrorism, active shooters in all sorts of locations, gang violence, inattentive drivers, lunatics, medical emergencies, and all sorts of accidents. These events can have unimaginable consequences and cost us our loved ones. We are not crazy; we are prepared to face reality that those who lost loved ones wish they had. We are prepared to face a reality that the untrained simply overlook because they don't see the world like we do. We are prepared to help those in need through times of disaster, loss, and hardship.

No one complains about "nuts" like us when we kill an active shooter the second they start firing at innocents. Imagine one of us had been around during these mass shootings and killed the perpetrator after his first victim. Imagine the loved ones that would still be here, had one of us been dropping our child off at Sandy Hook. In times like that, no one would complain about our presence and would thank us as heroes. Yet, while there is no emergency facing them, they look at us in a weird light. As if to say, "thanks for being severely messed up in combat to protect our nation, now could you please leave us alone, so we don't have to deal with your problems?" The "ordinary" feel threatened by us, almost ashamed that we are left as haunted minds that unsettle them.

We are the protectors for those who overlook reality, those who are blindfolded by social media. When Ukraine got invaded, do you remember seeing the men boarding trains to evacuate? In times of need, the men fled the area instead of fighting for their homes. These are prime examples of the blind, weakened by their contentment with a phone. Once things go awry, these are the people who look to "nuts" like us for guidance. They see our preparedness and our calm demeanor in the face of danger, they flock to us for stability. Make no mistake, there's plenty wrong with us but that is an asset. What haunts us, saves us. My reactions have saved my life in combat. When the moment calls for it, my reactions bring us all home safely. Those of us who are calm and collected in the face of chaos are the only reliable ones left.

Look back at the corona virus lockdowns. Remember how many people were out of basic supplies and food? Had they been prepared, they wouldn't have been in need. Look back at all of the protests and looting, the racial violence, and extremism across our nation. When things like that happen, the deindividuated mass does not care who it harms. The only thing guaranteeing your safety is your ability to notice the threat and repel it.

Mentality

We all walk through the valley of the shadow of death, but it is our choice not to make it out. Through a lifetime of struggle, we train for it. It may be dark and cold, but we have the choice to bring a flashlight and a jacket. It's also not mandated that we walk through the valley, it should be our instinct to run through it in order to minimize our exposure to the conditions. Yet, some continue to walk, feel sorry for themselves, and even break down into a crawl. Their pain will last long. Your perception of the valley is your reality. Your mentality is the difference between success and failure. It's only through hell that we learn our abilities.

As I row my boat down the river, I notice the waterfall fast approaching. In my panic, the river itself also changes into a stream of fire and think that there's no way out. This can't get any worse. Then, enemies set up on the riverbank and open fire on me, hitting me multiple times with their first burst. I slump over, defeated, as their fire continues to chew away at my smoldering boat. I look at my wounds, I'm bleeding strength, perseverance, intellect, wisdom, honesty, courage, charisma, benevolence, and philanthropy. Finally, in my dying moment, I see what has been coursing through my veins, what I was made of the whole time. The remaining slivers of boat plunge over the falls. I begin to soar like the albatross that I always was but never knew, for the world had convinced me that I was but a mouse.

The Humanity In Us All

You have no idea what darkness lies within you until having done it. We think we are better than others, but we truly do not know what our actions would be if we were in the circumstances that warranted their action. We are all human, having the same temptations of lust, murder, lying, stealing, cheating, swindling, substance abuse, all of humanity's faults lie within us all. The only determinant of who we are is our ability to keep resisting these temptations. Right and wrong are simply concepts of society, they're social norms. Those who disregard the social norm, though accepted in other areas, become branded as a criminal, anti-social, or a sociopath. People hide these desires at all costs, even from themselves. This becomes dangerous because those desires will come out when someone has the opportunity, believes they can act anonymously, believes they can get away unnoticed, or deindividuate as part of a group. Only then is their true self, their inner desire, known to them. They, along with all of us, hide behind our mask of composure, the inner self hides even from us. It is only when we recognize these desires and faults that we can truly know ourselves, to be the person that we actually need to be. A doctor cannot heal a wound that you deny having and you cannot grow yourself into a better person until you know who you really are. Except in cases of psychosis, severe delusion, and other reality altering mental disorders, it's constant that our learned "scripting" can be rewritten through effort, education, and social feedback. Yet, the ones who truly need the help do not seek it. They feed their delusion beast, live a skewed reality, and deny having any problem at all. "What we don't know, that's bad. What we don't know that we don't know, that's worse."

As far as judging goes, it will happen to you no matter what side of the fence you're on. People will always point the finger of shame to shift the blame, they point the finger to self-validate their learned principles. Do what you know in your heart is right, do what makes your family happy, and do what builds your relationships. You can only be convicted by your own heart. The right/wrong concept changes with ever changing social norms. Things such as promiscuous relationships, consuming alcohol, homosexuality, and eating a good old fashioned pulled pork sandwich can get you executed in lands where they execute unwanted wives, burn infidels, rape children, and practice misogyny as a norm. Both sides point the finger needlessly instead of minding their own business.

Personally, I believe in a Laissez Faire government and a principle of Give Me Liberty or Give Me Death. I live by my moral code and will defend my family against unwanted others. Either through diplomacy or conflict, it is our duty as men. "He who appeals to the law against his fellow man is either a fool or a coward. He who cannot take care of himself without that law is both." We cannot stand by idly, hoping for a lawman to come fight our battles. If someone harms your family, will it be a comfort to you knowing that the police will be there to report it within minutes? The damage is already done because you sat there doing nothing.

We are developing a society of the self-entitled. People can walk up to you and do or say whatever they want, no matter how vile. Someone could walk up and talk about raping your wife, you hit him in the mouth, and you're going to jail for it. They believe it's their right to do so. Is this justice? Certainly not. Yet in the eyes of the law, they'd rather you entered a civil suit. This is honorless injustice that plagues our once great nation. The nation where all men are created equal has become a racially driven mad house of disrespect and confusion.

Perhaps if we would incorporate a psychology program into our public education, we would have far less issues. If we could even have an hour each day dedicated to the betterment of society, we may see fast improvements and more so throughout the years. Yet, if we push these matters on the youth, some will argue that children are being brain washed and strongly reject the practice. We spend billions of dollars to militarize law enforcement agencies to respond once severely damaged people lash out, how much better would it be if we could educate the hatred and lack of understanding out of those damaged people? We've resorted to "prompt response and thorough investigation" after these atrocities happen but pay no attention as to why these things occur. Yet every time one of these mass shooters are in the news, they have that distinct look of a mad man. Their peers claim to have shown concern about them. The precursors are there. Our society allows endless bullying to occur until these injured people snap and kill everyone near them. They stand by idly, while in a position to help to the point of allowing these things to happen each day and they wonder why people snap. People hide behind the excuse of "it's not my responsibility." Well, you're a member of society and are allowing someone to be pushed to the point of murder. Who is really at fault here?

Seriousness

Being too serious in life can create chaos in the mind. You will begin dwelling on trivial things and the stress will consume you. Humor and happiness should be one of your priorities. Humor can make even the worst situations tolerable. Being too serious led me into delusion so much that my enjoyment of life was only possible if I could guarantee my safety. I saw threats everywhere, wouldn't leave the house without my pistol or two, and couldn't stand public events.

I was very serious about my military career as I blindly followed Pavlov's reward system. I was validated by others through awards and recognition. I was so serious that I hadn't noticed that I was in a pointless marriage, simply to uphold the appearance of stability and monogamous moral code. It was merely to show that I could be committed and live a stable life. Once this was attained, I was empty.

I was too distracted by my serious image to even know who I was as a person. I was so serious about my career that I was unable to see reality until after the rocket strike in Kabul. I thought to myself, what if I had died without meeting my daughter, without repairing damaged relationships, without finding who I really am? I would have been the body of a lost person. An empty shell of a man with a posthumous Purple Heart on my chest. I wouldn't have known what a true relationship is, but I would have had a medal. I wouldn't have been the person that I've grown to be, but I'd have a medal. I chased my career and only my career, letting every other area of my life become neglected. I was ignorant, closed minded, and only focusing on my next deployment.

That's how life slipped away from me, that's how much an image meant to me. Had it not been shattered abruptly, I would never have seen the error of my ways.

Where I Went Wrong

Through my pursuit of bravado and as a coping method from the immense stress, I let my emotion slip entirely from me. I became numb, nearly becoming an auto piloted drone. Situations that would cripple people emotionally, I went through with a stolid demeanor. I've always heard "if you lose your cool, you lose your command." Through death of family members, death of friends, divorce, combat, stopping a friend's suicide attempt, watching Mr. Bolton bleed out on LA-28 while unable to do anything but wait for the helicopter, feeling hot blood leaking into my hands, smelling the bodies in the Afghan heat, then federal prison, I retain my eerie calm. The MP who transported me to the MP station reflected in his report "Taylor was eerily calm and talkative as if nothing had happened" to my knowledge, nothing had happened at that point. It took several months for the Feds to finally tell me that something happened. Even then, there was no word of any injuries.

I try not to stress over things that I cannot change, I just simply adapt to an ever changing world. The events of life, whether good or bad, will happen with or without my emotional involvement. I knew this and allowed myself to become numb. I didn't care about anything, and my days became an endless cycle of training and drinking until right before I was arrested. I was living normally for about two months and then all of this shit happened. Happy recovery! Right?

Before incarceration, I was living the life of an all-purpose go-to guy. No matter what anyone needed, whether it be a few hundred mile road trip on Christmas Eve, suicide attempts, going through personal crisis, needed extraction from abusive relationships, or needed help kicking in doors at 3:07 in the morning, I was there. I've done wild things, to include putting myself in the line of fire, for those that I care about. Once life begins to slip from you, there's no telling where you will end up. Due to my shenanigans, I ended up in Federal Prison.

It's through times like this that I've realized that only we are responsible for ourselves. No one will help you but you. You must educate yourself, become self-reliant, and independent. Those around you should be doing the same. I've also learned never to get into a relationship with someone unless they're completely self-reliant. Only then will you know for sure that they're with you because they choose to be. If someone relies on you for anything, they'll play the role in order to get it.

Knowledge

Knowledge keeps you young. It's been long proven in every culture that the harder you have to work, the higher toll it takes on your body. Through knowledge of medicine, we learn to keep our teeth, cure and prevent disease, take care of our bodies, and properly feed ourselves. Knowledge of mathematics, physics, chemistry, and engineering helps us minimize effort during work and increase the strength of our homes. This saves pain, stress, and our bodies. Knowledge in psychology, sociology, and social psychology can help us coexist and work with each other more efficiently. It builds our tolerance and understanding of other cultures. Knowledge develops modern technology which brings the world together, overcome language barriers, and bridges the cultural gaps. Logistics, economics, agriculture, and customs keep people happily fed, clothed, employed, and supplied with luxuries. All of these keep the "hard work" to a minimum and preserve us. It is only through knowledge that we can advance as a species from what our ancestors were even decades ago. If we can have each generation increase their knowledge level even minutely, we will quickly see the world evolve.

Cultures that lack education, customs, and a stable society are rich in crime, ignorance, racism, and having low life expectancy. A warlord may be a reality that they face in daily life. Armed men come into power when the populace is too ignorant to see the flaws in their logic. Just as politicians do across civilized culture, warlords use charisma to skew reality to the point of genocidal hackings.

Look into the school environment. The same standardized testing process has become redundant. Our youth are learning more from phone applications than they are in structured education. The knowledge of the world is available to us at our fingertips. We can learn any subject, right now, and all you have to do is pull out your device. No matter how complex the task, the resource is right there. MIT has a phone application so you can learn nearly any subject. Several other colleges are following along and have K-12 programs listed by grade level and subject. Those who wish to read far ahead of their peers are no longer restricted by their grade level. We are finally free to learn as we please. What will you do with this opportunity?

As I've said before, the time is now. You should be sitting in your plate carrier, Glock 19 press checked and secured in your side holster, pen in hand, whatever you decide to do, whatever device you use, open to something meaningful. Whatever skill you are not fluent in, go learn from an educational video and put this to use. Was a certain subject a weak point for you through school? Get on an educational app and get good at it. You can only advance when you refuse to accept your weaknesses and do better. The clock is ticking, and your enemy is in school right now.

Learning ignorance, learning to hate you, learning how to kill you. Don't sit by idly and let them win.

Chapter 12

History Speaks

The men of history, whose words live on, deserve being repeated and passed through the generations.

The law obliges us to fight and die for liberty, and ordains that we should die for our parents, our friends, our children. All men are bound by these duties. But a higher duty is laid upon the sage; he must die for his principles and the truth he holds dearer than life. It is not the law that lays his choice up on him, it is not nature; It is the strength and courage of his own soul. Though fire or sword threaten him, it will not overcome his resolution or force him in the slightest of falsehood; But he will guard the secrets of others' lives and all that has been entrusted to his honor, as religiously as the secrets of initiation.

-Apollonius

Cowards die many times before their deaths; The valiant never taste of death but once. Of all the wonders that I yet have heard. It seems to me most strange that men should fear; Seeing that death, a necessary end, Will come when it will come.

-William Shakespeare

A human being should be able to change a diaper, plan an invasion, butcher a hog, con a ship, design a building, write a sonnet, balance accounts, build a wall, set a bone, comfort the dying, take orders, give orders, cooperate, act alone, solve equations, analyze a new problem, pitch manure, program a computer, cook a tasty meal, fight efficiently, and die gallantly. Specialization is for insects.

-Robert Heinlein

A clay pot sitting in the sun will always be a clay pot. It has to go through the white heat of the furnace to become porcelain.

-Mildred Witte Stouven

It's not a matter of who's going to let me, it's who's going to stop me.

-Ayn Rand

Doveryai No Proveryai- Trust, but verify

-Russian Proverb

Those who avoid war, welcome oppression. For it is they who saw it coming and allowed it to advance.

-RT

If you proclaim your own nonviolence, you will be a sitting duck for others---a chump.

-Jan Narveson

A cowardly man thinks he will ever live, if warfare he avoids, but old age will give him no peace, though spears may spare him.

-Odin

When I whet my flashing sword and my hand takes hold on judgment, I will reign vengeance upon my enemies; I will repay those who abased me.

-Deuteronomy 32:41

I will execute great vengeance upon them with furious rebukes; And they shall know that I am the Lord when I lay my vengeance upon them.

-Ezekiel 25:17

The Lord will come with fire, God's Chariots like a wild storm, to repay in hot anger, to rebuke with fiery flames. With fire and with sword the Lord will judge all humanity; Many will be slain by the Lord.

-Isaiah 66:15-16

Slay them wherever you find them; Drive them out of the places from which they drove you, for persecution is worse than killing. Fight them until there is no more Fitna and religion belongs to Allah alone.

-Al-Baqarah 190-193

The men and women of history speak great truths on nearly every subject and their words lead on for us to follow. These were some of them that I've copied down over the years. Once you realize that these phrases are the true insights to the spirit of humankind, you'll both be comforted and scared. Along the lines of what Ayn Rand said, I've noticed a great truth. The only thing stopping anyone from doing anything is the person who is willing to apply violence and risk their life to do so. Laws only provide a punishment after the crime if the person is caught. To stop anyone from doing anything to you or your family, you must stand your ground and be willing to kill that person should they persist. This is why I'm selective in my conflicts. If I have an issue with someone else's life, then it's my responsibility to force them to stop. Appealing to the law only adds confusion to the problems.

I hope that this has taught you, inspired you, cautioned you, and most importantly made you think about where your life is at. I hope that by learning through me, you can avoid the problems that I've run into and that your efforts are successful.

Contributions

Over the last 15 years, I've worked with outstanding leaders, mentors, coaches, friends, and role models that have taught me more than I'd ever be able to put into a book. I've kept my close acquaintances out of this section to protect their identities, but they know who they are. The wild men, the leaders, the thinkers, the builders, the strategizers, the operators, the drinking pals, and all those from the clubs down South. Thanks for all the good times.

A huge thank you must go out to all of my brothers and sisters in the 10th Mountain Division at Fort Polk and Fort Drum for sticking through all of the rough times that we endure at work. While on the subject of work, I must extend the same thank you to Customs and Border Protection's BMTF, the 519th Military Police Battalion, and all those who put their lives on the line to keep our domestic threats at bay. Thank you to the 509th at Fort Polk for all of the invaluable training experiences, both as RTU and as "augies."

Thank you to the 19th Special Forces Group and the 7th Special Forces Group for the countless hours of training, the knowledge gained on operations, and showing us all how to think outside the box. Your knowledge and experience has helped us all become better leaders, better war fighters, and better peers to each other.

Thank you to my friends that went on to become members of the 75th Ranger Regiment, you and your brothers endure some of the worst and you continue to get back in line for second helpings of the war sandwich. Thank you for doing all that you do and for your constant dedication to the cause.

To the crew at Darkness to Light, thank you for all you do and for the motivation that you provide other groups with similar goals. You've set the bar high for others to reach for and your operations make all the difference in the lives of those you rescue from hell. You are the spearhead of inspiration for many.

To the Domestic Abuse Response Team (DART), Safety Net for Abused Persons (SNAP), Chez Hope, Project Celebration, and the Dove programs abroad, thank you for the services you provide to many. Perhaps I'll have the pleasure pulling a trigger in the name of freedom for your organization.

A huge thank you must go out to the following gifted authors who inspired me over the years, taught me invaluable lessons, and showed me how to be more open minded. Thank you to Tim Macwelch, Gerald Rowan, Barry Davies, Pete Blaber, Annie Jacobsen, David Lambert, Joe Navarro, Phillipe Truchet, Jack Schafer, Robert Greene, David Craig, Simon Baron-Cohen, David Nash, Jeni Rogers, Doctor Julia Shaw, Carissa Veliz, John Carney, Herb Wade, James Wilkerson, Clint Emerson, Shoshana Zuboff, Jack Donovan, Mark Victor Hansen, Robert G. Allen, Gabrielle Bernstein, Deepak Chopra, Friedrich Nietzsche, Niccolò Machiavelli, Viktor Frankl, and Sun Tzu. You've produced wonderful work and have guided many readers like myself to open our minds to new possibilities. Some of you have brought me back to normal from the brink of absolute mental disarray and I can't thank you enough for being so open and confident with your words.

Thank you to all of my readers and followers. Your dedication to bettering yourselves to becoming a better person in society, your dedication to knowledge and your desire to secure a future for your family are my motivation to put out more books like this.